Bazel in Depth

Definitive Reference for Developers and Engineers

Richard Johnson

Contents

3

Introduction

Bazel is a powerful and extensible build system designed to handle the challenges of modern software development. It offers scalable, reproducible, and hermetic builds, making it well-suited for projects of varying sizes and complexity. This book, *Bazel in Depth*, provides a comprehensive exploration of Bazel's architecture, configuration, extension mechanisms, and performance optimization strategies, enabling practitioners to fully leverage its capabilities.

The core of Bazel is its build architecture, which revolves around a directed acyclic graph of dependencies. Through a rigorous understanding of targets, labels, packages, and actions, Bazel orchestrates complex builds deterministically. The underlying evaluation engine, Skyframe, offers precise computation caching and incremental evaluation, supporting fast and reliable build execution. Special emphasis is placed on hermeticity and sandboxing, ensuring builds are isolated from environmental inconsistencies and external side effects. This foundation guarantees reproducibility and security across diverse platforms.

Effective use of Bazel depends heavily on correctly structuring the configuration files that declare build rules and workspace dependencies. The BUILD and WORKSPACE files are central to defining targets, managing external dependencies, and organizing rules for large codebases. This book details syntax and semantics, as well as best practices for modularization, reusability through macros,

1

and fine-grained control over visibility and aliasing. Maintaining scalable and maintainable build definitions is critical to long-term project health.

Extending Bazel's functionality to meet specific project requirements is accomplished through Starlark, a Python-like language designed for writing custom build rules and repository definitions. Readers will find a thorough treatment of Starlark fundamentals, rule authoring, data propagation, and the strategic application of macros versus rules. The text also addresses performance considerations and robust testing and debugging techniques for Starlark extensions, essential for building reliable and maintainable custom workflows.

Dependency management and build optimization are crucial in large-scale systems. This volume explores sophisticated dependency graph analysis using Bazel query tools, and strategies to handle transitive and diamond dependencies efficiently. Managing external repositories at scale, version pinning, and cross-language builds are examined in detail. It also provides guidance for creating custom repository types and mirrors to improve reproducibility and security within complex build environments.

Performance and scalability are hallmarks of Bazel, which supports parallel and incremental builds as well as distributed execution. The book covers optimization of the action graph, profiling for bottleneck identification, and tuning remote execution and caching. Resource control under high concurrency and the challenges of scaling Bazel usage in monorepos and build farms are discussed thoroughly with proven architectural patterns and operational practices.

Testing forms an integral part of the Bazel ecosystem. The book presents an in-depth analysis of Bazel's built-in and third-party testing support, including the execution model, test isolation, parallelism, sharding, caching, and flakiness diagnosis. Coverage analysis and continuous integration with Bazel are explored to ensure high-quality and maintainable test suites. Readers are also guided on developing custom test rules for advanced scenarios.

Security, compliance, and reproducibility are increasingly important in modern software supply chains. This work provides detailed coverage of best practices for hermetic builds, sandboxing for attack surface reduction, automated dependency auditing, and cryptographic verification of build artifacts. Strategies for secrets management and integration of static and dynamic security analyses are presented to enhance trustworthiness in complex build pipelines.

Adopting and maintaining Bazel at scale requires careful planning and tooling. Practical approaches to migration from legacy build systems, incremental adoption, automated refactoring, and policy for upgrades and compatibility are examined. Maintaining custom rules in evolving environments and monitoring build health metrics complete this discourse, preparing teams to sustain Bazel usage effectively.

Finally, the book discusses future directions and open challenges in build engineering. It highlights experimental features in Bazel, adaptation to cloud-native and serverless contexts, applications of AI and machine learning for build and test optimization, and evolving community standards and best practices.

By providing a detailed and technical examination of Bazel's components and workflows, *Bazel in Depth* is intended for developers, build engineers, and technical leads seeking to master Bazel for complex software systems. Whether designing high-performance build infrastructures or developing custom extensions, readers will find authoritative guidance to support robust, efficient, and secure builds.

Chapter 1

Bazel's Core Architecture

Uncover what makes Bazel extraordinarily fast, scalable, and reliable. In this chapter, we open the hood on Bazel's foundational mechanisms—exploring how its rigorous build model, dependency graph, and caching strategies come together to deliver hermetic builds on fleets of machines. See why Bazel's core systems are trusted for some of the world's biggest codebases and understand the vital roles of isolation, reproducibility, and remote execution.

1.1. Fundamental Concepts and Terminology

The foundation of Bazel's build system is constructed upon a set of interrelated core concepts: *targets*, *labels*, *packages*, *rules*, and *actions*. Each represents a distinct abstraction within Bazel's model, collaboratively enabling precise, scalable, and reproducible builds. A clear understanding of these foundational elements is essential for comprehending Bazel's operational mechanics and ar-

5

chitecture.

Targets

A *target* is the fundamental unit of buildable or testable entities within Bazel. It is an individual build artifact or a logical grouping thereof that a developer can invoke via the build system. Targets typically correspond to outputs such as compiled binaries, libraries, or test suites. Conceptually, a target aggregates all the necessary inputs, dependencies, and instructions required to produce one or more outputs.

Targets are defined by *rules*, which specify how the target is built. For example, a target producing a Java binary may compile `.java` source files into `.class` files, package them, and link dependencies accordingly. The abstraction allows developers to focus on what needs to be built, not the intricate details of the build commands.

Labels

A *label* uniquely identifies a target within the Bazel workspace. It serves as a globally addressable reference used to declare dependencies and link targets together. Labels follow a structured syntax designed to unambiguously locate a target based on its package and name.

The canonical format for a label is:

```
//path/to/package:target_name
```

Here, `//` denotes the workspace root; `path/to/package` specifies the package relative path; and `target_name` is the name of the target within that package. The colon and target name can sometimes be omitted if the target name matches the package name, for conciseness.

For example:

```
//app/lib:utils
```

6

```
//third_party/boost:boost_system
//tools/build
```

Labels enable a precise and concise declaration of dependencies, forming the directed acyclic graph (DAG) on which Bazel bases its builds.

Packages

A *package* is a directory containing a set of related targets, governed by a single BUILD file, typically named BUILD or BUILD.bazel. The BUILD file systematically declares the targets and their associated rules. Packages provide modular boundaries, encapsulating source code, build logic, and metadata.

Within each package, targets can depend on one another using relative labels by omitting the package path:

```
cc_library(
    name = "foo",
    srcs = ["foo.cc"],
)

cc_binary(
    name = "foo_bin",
    deps = [":foo"],
)
```

In this example, the binary target foo_bin depends on the library foo within the same package, using the relative label ":foo".

Packages also encapsulate visibility rules that control accessibility of targets outside their package, supporting large-scale modularization and enforcing architectural boundaries in complex codebases.

Rules

Rules define the schema and logic used to produce targets. Each rule specifies what inputs it accepts, what outputs it produces, and the procedure for generating those outputs from the inputs. At the heart of Bazel's extensibility, rules enable support for multiple languages, platforms, and build scenarios.

Rules can be categorized as *built-in* or *custom*:

- **Built-in Rules:** Provided by Bazel natively for common languages and tools, such as `cc_library`, `java_binary`, `py_test`.

- **Custom Rules:** User-defined using Starlark, Bazel's extension language, enabling users to describe new types of build logic or workflows.

A typical rule definition includes attributes describing inputs (source files, dependencies), outputs (artifacts generated), and other metadata (visibility, licensing). Rules abstract away platform-specific commands, promoting portability and correctness.

Actions

An *action* is the indivisible build step executed by Bazel to generate outputs during a build. Actions take declared inputs-files or artifacts-and run commands that produce outputs. Together, actions form the edges of the build dependency graph.

Actions are typically the result of expanding rules into concrete shell commands or tool invocations. For example, compiling a C++ source file into an object file corresponds to one action. Linking object files into an executable is another. Bazel precisely tracks these actions, their inputs, and outputs, enabling intelligent incremental builds, caching, and parallel execution.

Each action is configured with the following:

- *Inputs:* Source files, generated files, or any dependencies required.

- *Outputs:* The generated artifacts produced.

8

- *Command:* The deterministic operation to be run, e.g., compiler invocation.

- *Environment:* Environment variables and execution context.

To illustrate, consider the compilation action for a C++ file:

```
inputs = ["foo.cc", "foo.h"]
outputs = ["foo.o"]
command = "g++ -c -o foo.o foo.cc"
```

This action takes the .cc and header files as inputs and produces the object file .o.

Interrelation and Build Graph

Targets, connected via labels, define dependencies forming a directed acyclic graph (DAG). Packages organize targets into logical units, while rules prescribe how targets are built. The build DAG's edges correspond to dependencies, and nodes correspond to targets.

Actions execute the concrete commands necessary to produce the outputs declared by these targets. The separation between *declaration* (targets and rules) and *execution* (actions) provides key advantages: incremental builds, parallelism, and hermeticity.

Summary of Core Concept Relationships

Concept	Role and Description
Target	Buildable/testable entity; aggregates inputs, dependencies, and build instructions.
Label	Unique identifier referencing a target; structured as //path/to/package:target_name.
Package	Directory with a BUILD file defining a set of targets; provides encapsulation.
Rule	Template specifying inputs, outputs, and commands; used to define target behavior.
Action	Atomic execution step performing command to produce outputs from inputs.

These abstractions collectively form Bazel's internal model

of building software, maintaining clarity, modularity, and determinism. Understanding these core concepts is vital for navigating Bazel's architecture and mastering advanced build configurations.

1.2. The Build Graph: Structure and Evaluation

Bazel organizes its build processes through an explicit representation of build dependencies in the form of a directed acyclic graph (DAG). This *build graph* powerfully encapsulates the complex interrelations among targets, enabling Bazel to perform precise incremental builds and to produce correct outputs deterministically.

At the core, a *target* in Bazel is a buildable entity such as a library, binary, test, or even a grouping of other targets. Each target corresponds to a node in the build graph; edges represent dependency relationships, pointing from dependents (consumers) to their dependencies (providers). This structure inherently precludes cycles, aligning well with the logical semantics of build dependencies where circular inclusion or consumption is nonsensical.

Each target declares its direct dependencies explicitly. These dependencies may include source files, other targets, or external repositories. The build rules and macros defined in Bazel's BUILD files specify these dependencies with exactitude. The graph node for a target encapsulates its associated metadata: inputs (files and dependent targets), outputs (generated artifacts), and the build action (command or script) responsible for producing outputs from inputs.

Consider an example simplified BUILD file snippet:

```
cc_library(
    name = "lib",
    srcs = ["lib.cc"],
    hdrs = ["lib.h"],
)
```

```
cc_binary(
    name = "app",
    srcs = ["app.cc"],
    deps = [":lib"],
)
```

Here, the binary target app depends on the library target lib, which itself depends on source files lib.cc and lib.h. The build graph creates an edge from the app node to lib, and further edges from lib to its source files.

When Bazel evaluates a build request, it begins with the specified target nodes and recursively traverses the graph in a post-order fashion. This means that a node's dependencies are evaluated first before the node itself. Such traversal ensures that all prerequisite artifacts are available before any dependent build actions execute.

During traversal, Bazel consults the cached build states of dependencies. If a dependency's outputs are already built and none of its inputs have changed, Bazel skips its rebuilding-a crucial optimization for incremental build efficiency. The traversal process supports lazy evaluation, only visiting nodes reachable from the build targets, which is critical when working with large projects having thousands of targets.

Bazel's evaluation strategy leverages the build graph's DAG structure to implement a highly precise incremental build mechanism. The state of each node in the graph is recorded, capturing the fingerprints of its inputs, outputs, and actions. During incremental builds, Bazel re-evaluates these fingerprints and compares them to cached values from previous builds.

If any input to a target (including transitive dependencies) has changed, Bazel marks the corresponding node as *dirty*. This prompts reevaluation and rebuilding of the target and its downstream dependents. Conversely, unmodified nodes remain cached, thereby avoiding unnecessary rebuilds.

This approach demands rigorous tracking of dependencies and inputs, down to metadata and command-line action parameters, to guarantee *correctness*. Any oversight in dependency declaration could lead to incomplete rebuilds and stale outputs. Bazel's model enforces strict dependency declarations, often verified during execution, to maintain graph integrity.

The acyclic nature of the build graph guarantees termination of traversal and evaluation. Cycles, if they existed, would cause infinite loops or inconsistent state. Instead, the DAG structure implies a partial ordering on build targets, facilitating parallelism: independent branches of the graph can be built concurrently without risk of race conditions.

Moreover, the DAG encapsulation facilitates advanced build features such as remote caching and distributed execution. By identifying dependency subgraphs and their fingerprints, Bazel can delegate portioned build execution or reuse artifacts built on remote systems.

The lifecycle of Bazel's build evaluation through the DAG can be summarized as follows:

1. Identify target nodes specified in the build invocation.

2. Recursively traverse the dependency graph in post-order.

3. For each node, compute input fingerprints based on source files, dependent outputs, and build actions.

4. Compare fingerprints to existing cache entries.

5. Rebuild nodes marked dirty; reuse cached outputs otherwise.

6. Propagate any changes upwards to dependent nodes.

7. Produce final outputs only after all dependencies have been successfully built.

This rigorous graph-driven evaluation mechanism ensures reproducibility and accuracy. The explicit, fine-grained representation of build dependencies coupled with the DAG structure affords Bazel a robust foundation for precise incremental builds, minimal rebuild work, and consistent artifact correctness in complex software projects.

1.3.   Skyframe: Underlying Evaluation Engine

Skyframe is the core computation engine that underpins Bazel's ability to efficiently handle complex builds through precise change tracking, smart caching, and extensive parallel execution. It represents a sophisticated directed acyclic graph (DAG)-based framework that models the build process as a series of interconnected, incremental computations. Each node in this graph corresponds to a discrete unit of work-the evaluation of a build artifact, query, or action output-while edges represent explicit dependencies among these computations. Understanding Skyframe's internal mechanisms is crucial to grasping how Bazel achieves high-performance and scalable builds under heavy codebase evolution.

At the heart of Skyframe lies its ability to maintain and update the evaluation state persistently and incrementally. The engine stores metadata and partial results of previous evaluations to minimize redundant recomputations. Whenever the build input or environment changes, Skyframe selectively invalidates only the affected nodes through precise dependency tracking. This fine-grained invalidation contrasts with traditional build systems that often resort to coarse-grained cache purging or full rebuilds. By recalculating only the minimal set of invalidated nodes, Skyframe ensures that Bazel achieves near-optimal rebuild times proportional to the actual change impact.

Skyframe models all build-related computations as nodes identified by unique keys. Each node can request the evaluation of other nodes through dependency edges. These dependencies are dynamic, allowing the evaluation graph to evolve as computations reveal additional dependencies during execution. Such dynamic dependency discovery enables complex build logic, such as conditional actions and rule-generated targets.

Each node in the graph maintains a state encapsulating:

- **Value:** The computed result of the node, e.g., a file artifact or build metadata.

- **Versioning:** Information about which state or snapshot of the inputs the computation corresponds to.

- **Invalidate Flags:** Indicators denoting whether the node's current computation is invalid with respect to the latest input versions.

- **Error and Exception States:** Data to represent and propagate failures encountered during computation.

This internal representation enables Skyframe to execute incremental builds by comparing input versions and selectively recomputing stale nodes. Notably, Skyframe employs a persistent graph structure that allows efficient reuse of prior computation results across separate Bazel invocations, reducing unnecessary disk I/O or redundant work even between clean starts.

Change tracking in Skyframe is facilitated by a sophisticated invalidation protocol tied to input versioning and dependency resolution. Inputs such as source files, environment variables, and external repositories are assigned version stamps. When an input changes, Skyframe marks all dependent nodes as invalid, triggering re-evaluation upon next access. The granularity at which changes propagate depends on explicit dependency edges; thus, the precision of the dependency graph directly impacts the efficiency of rebuilds.

Skyframe's invalidation engine incorporates the following core principles:

- **Deterministic dependency edges:** Each dependency is encoded explicitly as part of node evaluation, preventing implicit or hidden dependencies that could compromise correctness.

- **Lazy re-evaluation:** Nodes are only re-evaluated when their values are requested after invalidation, avoiding eager or unnecessary computations.

- **Error propagation:** Errors in dependencies cause dependent nodes to be invalid or fail evaluation, allowing early detection of faulty or inconsistent states.

This design ensures that incremental rebuilds are sound, reusing maximum available cached results, and that changes efficiently cascade through only affected build artifacts.

Skyframe's design inherently supports extensive parallelism, a vital feature for large-scale monorepos and distributed build environments. The build graph's DAG structure allows simultaneously evaluating all independent nodes concurrently while respecting explicit dependency constraints. To facilitate parallelism, Skyframe incorporates an execution scheduler that coordinates work assignments to threads or processes while maintaining determinism and consistency.

Key features enabling parallel execution include:

- **Fine-grained task decomposition:** Nodes represent minimal units of work for better load balancing across available resources.

- **Concurrent evaluation with dependency barriers:** Nodes are scheduled for execution only when all dependencies have completed successfully, enforcing correct build order.

- **Worker pools and asynchronous computation:** Skyframe leverages worker threads and non-blocking asynchronous evaluations to maximize CPU utilization and mitigate I/O bottlenecks.

- **Deterministic concurrent caching:** Caches and state stores used for memoization support concurrent reads and writes without compromising correctness.

Through these strategies, Skyframe achieves high throughput on multi-core and distributed setups, substantially shortening build latency compared to sequential or less optimized approaches.

Caching is foundational to Skyframe's performance. It implements memoization by associating computation results with node keys and their input versions. When a node with a known key and input version is requested, Skyframe retrieves its cached value without recomputing. The cache's scope extends beyond runtime memory caches to persistent on-disk stores, enabling cache reuse across Bazel invocations or even CI builds.

Skyframe supports advanced cache management techniques, such as:

- **Partial invalidation:** Retaining unaffected portions of cached results when a subset of dependencies change.

- **Garbage collection:** Periodically evicting outdated or unused node entries while preserving critical computation results.

- **Remote cache integration:** Allowing distributed caching systems to store and retrieve build outputs, dramatically reducing redundant execution.

Memoization within Skyframe is conceptually similar to functional programming's pure function caching, as nodes' values depend solely on their inputs and dependencies' results. This purity assumption is critical; any non-determinism or implicit side effects would compromise cache correctness and incremental build guarantees.

To illustrate Skyframe's operational flow, consider the incremental rebuilding of a target after a source file modification:

1. The modified source file is identified; its version number increments.

2. Skyframe traverses the graph, marking all nodes directly or indirectly dependent on this file as invalid.

3. Upon request for the target's value, Skyframe initiates re-evaluation:

   - Dependency nodes not invalidated or unchanged return cached values immediately.

   - Invalidated nodes execute their associated computation functions, potentially adding new dependencies.

4. Evaluations proceed in parallel where dependencies allow, with synchronization points ensuring correct ordering.

5. Results are memoized associating updated node versions to their computed values.

6. Build actions driven by Skyframe's evaluated nodes generate new output artifacts.

This incremental and parallel approach ensures that Bazel's rebuild time is closely proportional to the actual impact of modifications on the build graph, minimizing redundant computation and resource usage.

Skyframe's architecture embodies a carefully designed synthesis of immutable data structures, precise dependency management, persistent state, incremental evaluation, and scalable concurrency. Together, these characteristics empower Bazel to handle large codebases with frequent changes, complex build dependencies, and heterogeneous artifact types efficiently. As a foundational component, Skyframe elevates Bazel beyond traditional build systems by offering superior correctness guarantees and performance through principled engineering of computation and change propagation.

1.4. Hermeticity and Reproducibility

Bazel's design philosophy centers on producing *hermetic* and *reproducible* builds, crucial properties for ensuring consistent outputs regardless of the build environment. Hermeticity refers to the complete isolation of build actions from external, uncontrolled influences such as environment variables, system-installed libraries, or transient filesystem state. Reproducibility ensures that two builds with identical inputs produce bitwise identical outputs, an essential facet for caching, debugging, and validating software artifacts.

The cornerstone of Bazel's approach to hermeticity lies in its rigorous enforcement of *hermetic inputs*. Each build action-typically a command that transforms input files into output files-receives its inputs and dependencies explicitly declared in the build graph. These include source files, generated files, tools, and runtime dependencies. This declaration allows Bazel to precisely identify and package all data required for execution, preventing implicit reliance on system-wide resources. By forbidding implicit file accesses, Bazel eliminates variability stemming from differences in programmers' machines, build servers, or continuous integration environments.

One core technique Bazel employs is the use of *sandboxed execution environments*, which effectively simulate a clean and minimal filesystem. Each compilation or test action runs inside a sandbox that presents only the declared inputs and required tools; no access exists to user home directories, global system libraries, or any extraneous files. This sandboxing ensures that environment variables such as PATH or locale settings cannot silently affect behavior. Bazel constructs the sandbox by bind-mounting declared inputs into place, using kernel features where available (e.g., Linux namespaces or Mac OS sandboxing APIs) or fallback strategies on other platforms. Consequently, developers are guaranteed that builds are reproducible and invariant to system configuration or transient states like caches or temporary files.

Closely tied to hermeticity is the requirement for *deterministic outputs*. Even within a hermetic sandbox, build actions can produce non-deterministic outputs due to factors like timestamps embedded in compiler-generated files, non-deterministic ordering of linked objects, or randomized identifiers. Bazel promotes deterministic builds through multiple mechanisms. First, it encourages using tools and compilers that support reproducible builds by suppressing embedded timestamps, fixing UUIDs, and providing stable data ordering. Second, Bazel itself canonicalizes output artifacts wherever possible by normalizing metadata such as modification times and ownership information during caching and storage. The content-addressed storage model used by Bazel's remote cache and execution systems hinges on deterministic artifacts, thus requiring careful treatment of these nuances.

Bazel's *build graph*, a directed acyclic graph of actions and dependencies, forms the backbone for both hermeticity and reproducibility. Each node corresponds to a deterministic action with well-defined inputs and outputs. Because Bazel hashes inputs to determine cache keys, even minor differences in input content or action definitions lead to cache misses, prompting re-execution. This mechanism encourages developers to declare dependencies accurately and maintain clean, hermetic build definitions. It also enables fine-grained incremental builds, only rebuilding affected targets.

To further isolate builds from system variations, Bazel locks down environments via *toolchains* and *platforms*. Toolchains specify exact compiler versions, flags, and environment variables that are consistent across build environments. Instead of implicitly invoking the system's default compiler or linker, Bazel explicitly controls tooling through configured toolchains, which can be hermetically packaged and versioned. Platforms describe the target architecture and operating system, ensuring the build logic correctly accounts for platform-specific details without accidental contamination. This controlled environment abstraction eliminates subtle discrepancies arising from heterogeneous environments.

Another dimension where Bazel enforces reproducibility is in *source manifests*. Instead of relying on wildcard globbing or implicit source discovery, Bazel requires explicit input declarations with full knowledge of input paths and contents. This eliminates surprises caused by adding or removing files unnoticed by the build definitions. The source manifest approach also facilitates precise dependency analysis and caching.

When remote caching or remote execution are employed, hermeticity and reproducibility become even more critical. Since remote workers often run in environments wholly outside developer control, Bazel's strict input declaration, sandboxing, and deterministic output guarantees ensure that remote builds remain consistent with local builds. This portability contributes to seamless scaling of large codebases and reduces the incidence of hard-to-debug "works on my machine" failures.

Bazel enforces environment-independent, reproducible builds through a combination of hermetic inputs, sandboxed execution, deterministic output production, explicit dependency declarations, and controlled toolchain abstractions. These measures collectively guarantee that identical inputs yield identical outputs, fostering reliable incremental builds, efficient caching, and scalable distributed build systems. The resulting reproducibility reduces developer friction, increases confidence in build correctness, and forms the foundation for robust software delivery pipelines.

1.5. Build Sandboxing and Isolation

Bazel's build sandboxing model is fundamental to its ability to produce hermetic, reproducible builds by isolating compilation and other build actions from the host environment. This model encapsulates each build action within a controlled environment that strictly limits access to only the declared inputs and prevents unintended side effects on the filesystem or other system resources. The sandboxing infrastructure acts as a gatekeeper, ensuring that build steps neither pollute the host environment nor depend on extraneous files, which directly translates into enhanced security, reliability, and consistency.

At the core of Bazel's sandboxing is the concept of a build action executed inside a minimal virtualized environment, commonly referenced as a "sandbox." The sandboxing system constructs an isolated workspace for every action: input files are localized into this workspace, outputs are written within it, and the command is executed with a carefully restricted view of the filesystem.

The architecture revolves around three main components:

- **Input materialization:** Only explicitly declared input files and directories are made available to the sandboxed process. Bazel copies or symlinks these inputs into the sandbox environment, ensuring strict control over what the build action can read.

- **Filesystem isolation:** Write operations by the process are constrained to the sandbox's ephemeral output directories. Any attempt to write outside these directories results in sandbox violation errors or access denials.

- **Process isolation:** The sandbox restricts environment variables and file descriptors to further reduce dependencies on the host environment, raising reproducibility and security guarantees.

The sandbox directory layout is carefully structured to mimic the expected workspace locations of inputs and outputs while preventing escape to the underlying system directories.

Implementing sandboxing consistently across multiple platforms—Linux, macOS, and Windows—presents significant challenges, given the differences in operating system capabilities for process and filesystem isolation.

Linux

On Linux, Bazel leverages native kernel features such as `namespace` isolation, `seccomp` filters, and `pivot_root` or `mount namespaces` to achieve strong sandboxing. Namespaces isolate the process's view of the filesystem, process IDs, network, and other resources. The sandbox process operates within a custom mount namespace where input directories are bind-mounted as read-only, and outputs are mounted private, preventing side effects on the system mount table. `seccomp` filters further restrict the system calls available to the build process, preventing operations outside the sandbox's permitted scope.

macOS

macOS lacks the same namespace features but offers `sandbox-exec` and macOS-specific `Seatbelt` profiles for confinement. Bazel's macOS sandboxing thus uses a hybrid approach: inputs are symlinked into a dedicated working directory, and `sandbox-exec` enforces restrictions on filesystem and network access through predefined profiles. This approach

22

prevents unauthorized file reads and writes but does not provide as strong isolation as Linux namespaces. Consequently, some build actions dependent on fine-grained system call interception may witness relaxed sandbox guarantees.

Windows

Windows sandboxing leverages `Job Objects` and `Filesystem Redirectors` to restrict processes. Bazel creates isolated temporary directories and symlinks input files into the sandbox. Job Objects constrain process resource usage and lifetime, while filesystem permissions and access control lists (ACLs) enforce read-only or write-access restrictions. Recent Windows versions also introduce features like `Windows Sandbox` and `AppContainer` for stronger isolation, though Bazel primarily depends on more lightweight file and process isolation techniques to support fast incremental builds.

Sandboxing significantly enhances build security by minimizing the attack surface that build actions may exploit. By forbidding build steps from reading arbitrary files or writing outside their output trees, Bazel ensures that injection of malicious code or leakage of sensitive information through side channels is vastly reduced. Environment control eliminates non-declared dependencies on system libraries or environment variables, which could cause nondeterministic behaviors or hide subtle vulnerabilities.

From a reliability standpoint, sandboxing prevents one build action from corrupting the outputs or inputs of another by enforcing strict write isolation. This isolation enables parallel builds and caching mechanisms to operate confidently without risking interference or race conditions. Moreover, it guarantees build hermeticity: the same inputs always produce identical outputs, regardless of host configuration. This reproducibility is crucial in large-scale monorepos and distributed build farms, where consistency across developer machines, continuous integration servers, and production environments is paramount.

While the sandboxing model greatly improves build correctness, it requires explicit declaration of all inputs, including indirect dependencies like header files or runtime resources. Failure to declare inputs results in build failures or erroneous sandbox violations, surfacing latent dependency issues and compelling more disciplined build specification.

Sandboxing can introduce overhead due to filesystem operations for input localization and output materialization. Bazel mitigates this with optimizations such as symlink farms instead of deep copies and caching of virtualized file structures. Nevertheless, very large inputs or file trees can still impact build latency.

Some build tools, especially those that embed custom runtime environments, invoke dynamic code loading or require network access, which sandboxing restricts by design. Bazel supports fine-tuned exemptions and configurable sandbox profiles to accommodate such cases while maintaining overall isolation policies.

Bazel's build sandboxing and isolation form the backbone of its robust, hermetic build system. By architecting an environment where build actions operate in strict confinement-with explicit inputs, controlled filesystem views, and process restrictions-Bazel achieves reproducibility, security, and parallelizability. These features distinguish it from traditional build systems, making it well-suited for complex, distributed, and security-sensitive build environments across diverse computing platforms.

1.6. Caching Mechanisms and Strategies

Caching in Bazel is a foundational technique that drives its ability to deliver fast, incremental, and reproducible builds at scale. The primary distinction lies between *local* caching, which leverages artifacts stored on the developer's machine or build cluster nodes, and *remote* caching, which utilizes shared, networked cache storage accessible across multiple machines or build agents. The interplay between these types, and the intricate design of cache keys and invalidation logic, form the basis for maximizing build performance and reliability.

Local Caching

Local caching persists build outputs—generated artifacts such as compiled object files, intermediate targets, and test results—directly on the local filesystem. When a build is triggered, Bazel consults the local cache to determine if the required outputs exist and are valid. This avoids redundant computation by reusing cached outputs when the build inputs and execution environment remain unchanged.

The local cache is highly efficient in single-developer or monolithic build environments with relatively stable workspaces. It minimizes disk I/O and network latency by accessing cache entries directly. However, local cache size is limited by disk capacity, and it is susceptible to cache loss if the local environment is wiped or corrupted.

Remote Caching

Remote caching extends this concept by storing build artifacts in a distributed cache service. This service can be accessed concurrently by multiple builders, enabling artifact reuse across developers, continuous integration (CI) systems, and build farms. Remote caching decouples cache storage from local environments, enhancing cache availability and storage scalability.

A key remote cache feature is *cache sharing*, enabling cross-machine reuse of artifacts. This is particularly beneficial in CI environments, where repeated builds occur on fresh agents or containers without local cache priming. Remote caching must therefore emphasize secure, consistent, and concurrent access controls to prevent cache corruption and ensure artifact integrity.

Cache Keys and Hashing

The cache key is essential to the effectiveness of Bazel's caching mechanism. It uniquely identifies build outputs and ensures their correctness upon reuse. Bazel computes these keys by hashing a combination of several factors:

- **Input content hashes:** All source files, dependency files, and toolchains that influence the target.

- **Build configuration:** Compiler flags, environment variables, and feature flags that impact the build behavior.

- **Action commands:** The commands or scripts executed during build steps, ensuring that changes therein trigger cache invalidation.

- **Platform-specific properties:** Architecture, operating system, and environment settings that may affect the produced artifacts.

By constructing a hash digest from these components, Bazel creates a deterministic and collision-resistant cache key. When a build action is invoked, this key is computed and checked against cache entries to locate reusable outputs.

Invalidation Logic

Cache invalidation ensures that stale or incompatible artifacts are not reused across builds. Bazel's invalidation logic hinges on cache key changes; if any input affecting the key differs from the previous build, the cache entry is deemed invalid.

Invalidation can be triggered by:

- **Source code modifications:** Changes in one or more files involved in the target.

- **Configuration drift:** Alterations in compiler settings, environment variables, or flags impacting build artifacts.

- **Action changes:** Modifications to build scripts or commands executed.

- **Dependency updates:** Updates in upstream targets or libraries.

Bazel employs a fine-grained dependency tracking system, which allows highly selective invalidation, minimizing rebuild scope. This reduces unnecessary computation and retains maximal cache utility while preserving correctness.

Strategies for Exploiting Cache Features

To maximize build speed and reliability using Bazel's caching capabilities, certain strategies can be employed:

1. Maximize Cache Hit Rates

Ensuring cache hits requires maintaining deterministic builds and minimizing non-deterministic state. This includes:

- Avoiding non-hermetic dependencies such as random number generation or timestamps in build actions.

- Using strict sandboxing or containerization to isolate builds from external state.

- Defining explicit inputs and outputs for all actions.

High cache hit rates reduce the need to re-execute expensive build steps, considerably accelerating incremental builds.

2. Leverage Remote Cache Sharing

Enabling remote caching in multi-developer or CI environments allows artifact reuse beyond local boundaries, decreasing build times dramatically.

Best practices include:

- Configuring reliable and high-throughput cache servers or services.

- Ensuring security policies around remote cache access.

- Balancing cache write and read bandwidth to avoid bottle-necks.

3. Fine-Tune Cache Granularity

Structuring Bazel targets to encapsulate logical build units with limited and well-defined dependencies maximizes cache efficiency. Smaller, isolated targets produce granular cache entries that are more frequently reusable.

Conversely, overly large targets reduce the opportunity for partial rebuilds and increase invalidation scope.

4. Avoid Cache Pollution

Cache pollution occurs when transient or invalid outputs overwrite correct cache entries, leading to incorrect reuse or cache churn. Strategies include:

- Utilizing Bazel's `local_cache_cleaner` tool to periodically maintain cache health.

- Avoiding build steps that produce non-reproducible outputs or side effects.

- Monitoring cache hit/miss rates through Bazel's profiling and logging tools.

5. Integrate Cache Warm-Up Techniques

Pre-populating caches in CI runners or developer machines with common artifacts, via artifact bundles or previous build snapshots, accelerates cold-start performance. Bazel supports cache upload and download commands simplifying this process:

```
bazel fetch //...
bazel build --remote_cache=http://cache-server ...
```

```
INFO: Remote caching enabled.
INFO: Artifact downloaded from cache: //lib:core
INFO: Build completed successfully
```

This avoids repeated cold builds on clean environments.

Bazel's caching design—anchored by local and remote caches, robust cache key computation, and rigorous invalidation—enables scalable, reliable, and performant builds. Optimizing both cache usage and target granularity, alongside leveraging remote cache sharing and managing cache health, unlocks substantial developer productivity gains. Understanding and applying these mechanisms is pivotal for maximizing Bazel's powerful build acceleration capabilities in complex engineering workflows.

1.7. Remote Execution Architecture

Bazel's remote execution architecture is designed to offload build actions to a network of remote workers, enabling scalable, efficient, and reproducible builds across distributed and cloud-native environments. This architecture decouples local build coordination from resource-intensive action execution, facilitating high concurrency and workload sharing, which is critical for large-scale software development projects.

At the core of Bazel's remote execution strategy lies a protocol that rigorously defines interactions between the client (Bazel build system) and the remote executors. This protocol is grounded in the Remote Execution API (REAPI), an open standard specifying key components: *Action, Command, Digest,* and *ExecutionRequest/Response.* These elements collectively orchestrate the remote execution lifecycle, ensuring consistency and traceability of build actions.

An *Action* encapsulates a single atomic build step, corresponding to a command line invocation. It references the command to execute, input file digests, platform requirements, and output metadata. The *Command* message details the executable, flags, environment variables, and working directory. Both *Action* and *Command* are identified by their content-addressable digests (typically SHA-256 hashes), ensuring immutability and deterministic identification of inputs and commands.

The remote execution workflow proceeds as follows:

1. **Input Preparation and Upload:** The client computes the digest of the *Action* and related *Command*, along with all input files' content digests. Inputs are uploaded to the remote Content Addressable Storage (CAS) if not already present, avoiding redundant data transfers.

2. **Execution Request Submission:** An *ExecutionRequest* is sent to a remote execution scheduler or direct executor. This request references the *Action* digest and includes execution parameters such as platform constraints (e.g., OS, CPU architecture).

3. **Remote Action Execution:** The remote worker retrieves inputs from the CAS, reconstructs the environment, and executes the action. The execution environment is ephemeral and isolated to guarantee reproducibility. Upon completion, output files and the command's exit status are captured.

4. **Output Upload and Response:** Output artifacts are uploaded back to the CAS, and an *ExecutionResponse* is returned to the client containing output digests, exit codes, and optional standard output/error streams.

5. **Result Caching and Reuse:** The Bazel client compares

the received outputs against previous results and caches them locally to accelerate subsequent builds. Remote caches may also interact with multiple clients, enabling cross-user cache sharing and further build time reduction.

The relationship between remote execution and caching is symbiotic. The CAS acts as a cloud-native artifact repository storing inputs and outputs in an immutable manner keyed by their content digests. Combined with the action cache component, this enables Bazel to exploit fine-grained cache hits with precision at the action level rather than entire builds or coarse artifacts.

Ensuring reliability and correctness in remote execution demands several architectural and operational considerations. First, remote workers must provide hermetic isolation of environments to avoid contamination or nondeterministic behavior from shared state. This is often enforced through containerization or sandboxing technologies, compatible with the *Action*'s platform specification.

Secondly, robust fault tolerance mechanisms are imperative, as network failures, node crashes, or timeouts commonly occur in distributed systems. Bazel's remote execution client includes retry logic and supports deadline-based expirations encouraged by the REAPI. This approach minimizes the impact of transient failures and maintains build stability.

Thirdly, security and access controls are essential, particularly in multi-tenant cloud environments. Authentication, authorization, and encryption protect build inputs, outputs, and metadata. The openness of the REAPI facilitates integration with standard identity management and secret distribution systems employed in enterprise infrastructures.

Use cases for Bazel's remote execution span both on-premises distributed compute clusters and cloud providers offering fully managed services. In distributed environments, organizations deploy pools of dedicated remote workers, leveraging existing infrastructure to reduce build latency and maximize resource utilization. Cloud-native deployments, conversely, benefit from elastic scaling and global availability, dynamically provisioning execution capacity as build demand fluctuates.

The flexibility of Bazel's architecture also supports hybrid scenarios combining local execution with prioritized remote offloading. This allows developers to run cache hits locally instantaneously while offloading more expensive or cache-miss actions remotely. Moreover, fine-grained cache invalidation and consistency guarantee that changes propagate correctly, avoiding stale build artifacts.

An example of a remote execution specification snippet in Bazel's configuration is shown below:

```
build --remote_executor=grpc://remote-exec.example.com:8980
build --remote_cache=grpc://remote-cache.example.com:8980
build --remote_timeout=300
build --remote_upload_local_results=true
build --experimental_remote_download_minimal=true
```

This configuration directs Bazel to connect to remote services using the gRPC protocol, setting timeouts and controls for how local results integrate with the remote caching infrastructure. The use of `--experimental_remote_download_minimal` minimizes unnecessary downloads, optimizing network bandwidth and local storage.

Observability and metrics are equally important. Remote execution systems emit granular telemetry such as queueing delays, execution durations, cache hit/miss rates, and error counts. These data streams are invaluable for troubleshooting, performance tuning, and capacity planning.

Bazel's remote execution architecture enables robust offloading of build actions via a protocol-driven, content-addressed model that integrates seamlessly with distributed and cloud-native environments. Its design addresses the demands of scalability, reliability, and security, unlocking accelerated build times and consistent developer experiences at scale.

Chapter 2

BUILD and WORKSPACE Files: Structure and Best Practices

These files are the living blueprint of any Bazel project—shaping, organizing, and controlling your builds at every scale. This chapter pulls apart the anatomy of BUILD and WORKSPACE files, demystifies best practices for complex codebases, and gives you the architectural tools to tame even sprawling monorepos. Master these artifacts, and you master Bazel's power to orchestrate large, elegant, and maintainable builds.

2.1. BUILD File Syntax and Semantics

The core component of Bazel's build system is the BUILD file. These files articulate the definition of build targets, encapsulating both their dependencies and the rules that govern their construction. Understanding the syntax and semantics of BUILD files is essential for crafting robust and maintainable build definitions. This section examines the fundamental elements of BUILD files, the structure and use of rules and targets, and the manner in which Bazel interprets these constructs during execution.

At their basis, BUILD files are written in Starlark, a subset of Python designed for build configuration. This language choice confers familiarity and flexibility while remaining deterministic and hermetic. A BUILD file consists of a sequence of rule invocations and function calls, without explicit control flow structures like loops or conditionals. Each rule defines one or more build targets by specifying attributes such as source files, dependencies, and output names.

Rules have the general form:

```
<rule_name>(
    <attribute1> = <value1>,
    <attribute2> = <value2>,
    ...
)
```

Each declared target is uniquely identified by a label, which by convention follows the format //package:path/to:target, where the package corresponds to the directory containing the BUILD file. Targets are implicit within rule calls; each rule invocation is associated with one or more target labels derived from the name attribute or default naming conventions.

Rules serve as parameterized templates encoding how to transform specified inputs into desired outputs. Bazel ships with a set of predefined rules, such as cc_library, java_binary, and py_test, which represent common build scenarios. Rules consist of declared attributes encompassing:

- **Sources**: The input files, typically enumerated by srcs.

- **Dependencies**: Other targets on which the current target depends, specified via `deps`.

- **Outputs**: Files produced by the build; often implicit but explicitly specifiable.

- **Name**: A mandatory identifier that distinguishes the target within the package.

For example, a C++ library rule might be expressed as:

```
cc_library(
    name = "mylib",
    srcs = ["foo.cc", "bar.cc"],
    hdrs = ["foo.h", "bar.h"],
    deps = ["//third_party/lib:util"],
)
```

Here, `mylib` is the target name. The `srcs` attribute provides the source files implementing the library, while `deps` lists external targets required during compilation.

Custom rules can also be defined using Starlark functions and macros, enabling encapsulation of build logic for specialized or composite targets. Such functions typically invoke existing rules or incorporate complex attribute manipulation to streamline BUILD file authoring.

Functions in BUILD files are written in Starlark and facilitate abstraction and reuse. Unlike rules, these functions do not produce build targets directly but generate rule invocations or manipulate data. Macros are a common pattern where Starlark functions emit one or more rule calls for ergonomic target bundling.

For instance, a macro might encapsulate a common pattern such as:

```
def my_cc_library_macro(name, srcs, hdrs, deps):
    native.cc_library(
        name = name,
        srcs = srcs,
        hdrs = hdrs,
        deps = deps,
    )
```

When invoked, `my_cc_library_macro` expands to a `cc_library` rule call. This layering enhances clarity and consistency within large-scale `BUILD` files.

Once `BUILD` files are parsed, Bazel translates the rules, targets, and function calls into an internal dependency graph. This graph represents all entities and their interrelations across the entire workspace. Bazel's build engine queries this graph during execution to determine necessary actions to produce or verify artifacts.

Key semantic principles underlie this process:

- **Determinism**: Each rule invocation yields targets with precisely defined inputs and outputs. Given identical inputs and environment, builds produce identical outputs, enabling caching and incremental builds.

- **Immutability**: Targets once defined in `BUILD` files are immutable within a build invocation. Changes to `BUILD` files require a new analysis phase, ensuring stability during execution.

- **Visibility and Scopes**: Targets declare their visibility, controlling which other packages or targets may depend on them. This encapsulation restricts unintended coupling and fosters modularity.

- **Label Resolution**: Bazel resolves labels to actual targets, considering repository mappings, package structures, and default behaviors for unspecified attributes.

- **Attribute Evaluation**: Attributes are evaluated in order, with default values supplied when omitted. Certain attributes accept computed values derived from other attributes or environment variables.

- **Rule Implementation**: The semantic meaning of a rule derives from its implementation in either native code or Starlark extensions. The rule defines how inputs map to outputs and the commands invoked, abstracting away execution specifics from BUILD files.

Conceptually, Bazel's analyzer constructs a detailed graph

$$G = (V, E)$$

where vertices V correspond to targets and edges E represent dependencies. Because of the declarative nature of BUILD files, this graph is static and acyclic at execution time, facilitating parallelism and incremental build strategies.

Mastering the syntax and semantics of BUILD files empowers developers to author build configurations that are:

- **Explicit**: All inputs, outputs, and dependencies are clearly declared, avoiding hidden side effects.

- **Composable**: Using macros and functions promotes reuse and reduces duplication.

- **Isolated**: Visibility controls ensure clean interfaces between components.

- **Scalable**: The static dependency graph enables Bazel's efficient parallel scheduling and cache utilization.

BUILD files provide a deterministic, declarative interface to specify complex build scenarios. Through a combination of rule definitions, target declarations, and Starlark abstractions, Bazel constructs an accurate model of the build universe. Understanding these file formats and their underlying semantics is foundational for harnessing the full capabilities of Bazel in large-scale, multi-language projects.

2.2. WORKSPACE Files and External Dependencies

In modern build systems, particularly those designed for large-scale and polyglot projects, the management of external dependencies and the definition of clear project boundaries are critical to maintainability, reproducibility, and modularity. The WORKSPACE file stands at the center of this mechanism, serving as an explicit declaration of the project boundary and as the point of integration for all external code repositories and tools needed for the build.

The WORKSPACE file is a specialized file residing at the root of a project's directory tree. Its primary role is to mark the root directory as a distinct project boundary and instruct the build system about the external resources upon which the project depends. When the build system processes a workspace, it recognizes that all build targets within the tree belong to a single project context, resolving references accordingly and isolating the project from other unrelated builds on the system.

By placing a WORKSPACE file at the root of the source tree, the build system treats the directory and all of its descendants as a cohesive unit. This demarcation prevents unintended cross-references between projects that may reside within a larger monorepository or filesystem. Furthermore, this project boundary ensures that command invocations for building and testing are relative and scoped correctly. The WORKSPACE file, even if empty, explicitly signals the existence of the workspace.

The essential function of the WORKSPACE file beyond project boundary definition is to specify external dependencies. These dependencies might include third-party libraries, tools, or services that the project requires. Rather than embedding or manually copying external source code directly into the project repository, the WORKSPACE file declares them formally, allowing for centralized management, version control, and isolation.

Dependencies can be specified through several repository rules, depending on the nature and location of the external resource:

- `http_archive` and `http_file` provide mechanisms to fetch remote archives or files via HTTP(S) URLs.

- `git_repository` and `git_commit` fetch dependencies directly from Git repositories, optionally pinned to specific branches, tags, or commits.

- `local_repository` allows local paths outside the main workspace directory to be referenced.

- `new_local_repository` and other domain-specific rules enable integration with proprietary or enterprise source systems.

A critical best practice when managing external dependencies is to pin them to deterministic versions. This practice ensures that builds are reproducible and invariant over time, avoiding issues such as transitive dependency drift and unexpected breakages when upstream projects change.

An example `WORKSPACE` snippet demonstrating a pinned HTTP archive dependency is shown below:

```
http_archive(
    name = "protobuf",
    urls = ["https://github.com/protocolbuffers/protobuf/releases
    /download/v3.21.12/protobuf-all-3.21.12.tar.gz"],
    sha256 = "
    e5b749b1f9838cdc4e85fd1a019c1b20304541af9a09626b5a53178b69a229a3
    ",
)
```

Here, the `http_archive` rule downloads a specific version of the Protocol Buffers library, identified both by its download URL and by a SHA-256 checksum. The checksum confirms the integrity of the downloaded archive, preventing issues caused by corrupted downloads or tampering. This form of explicit versioning and verification is paramount for stringent build reproducibility.

41

For dependencies sourced from Git repositories, a pinned commit hash is preferred:

```
git_repository(
    name = "grpc",
    remote = "https://github.com/grpc/grpc.git",
    commit = "8e6f5f7797a84a0a49c770890509d3b2800bbde9",
)
```

This guarantees that the exact state of the repository at the specified commit is used in the build, mitigating variability.

The WORKSPACE file facilitates modular dependency definition, but managing multiple interconnected dependencies introduces complexity. Transitive dependencies—dependencies of dependencies—can cause version conflicts or duplication if not carefully controlled.

Frequently, projects use "dependency constraints" or "aliasing" to unify versions or exclude problematic transitive dependencies. Although these are often handled at the build target level via BUILD files or supplementary configuration files, the WORKSPACE file remains the single source of truth for the foundational external dependency versions.

By explicitly declaring all external dependencies within the WORKSPACE file, the build system can fetch and cache these dependencies in a controlled environment. This supports hermetic builds: builds that produce identical outputs regardless of the host environment or underlying system state. Since all third-party code is versioned and integrated from declared sources, builds are reproducible and modular. This approach is vital for continuous integration, deployment pipelines, and security audits.

- **Explicit Project Boundaries:** WORKSPACE defines the root, delineating project scope and preventing ambiguous dependency resolution.

- **Versioned External Integrations:** Pinned third-party

dependencies ensure reproducible builds by avoiding floating references.

- **Reproducibility and Caching:** Precise declarations enable caching of dependencies and offer hermetic build environments.

- **Modularity:** Clear definition of external libraries and tools supports incremental builds and modular growth.

- **Security:** Checksums and pinned versions reduce the risk of supply-chain attacks and compromised dependencies.

The WORKSPACE file serves not only as a boundary marker but as a comprehensive manifest for external dependencies. The disciplined specification and management of these dependencies are a cornerstone of robust software engineering practices in advanced build systems.

2.3. Rule Declaration and Organization

Effective rule declaration and organization are essential for managing complex build configurations, particularly in large-scale software projects. The strategies employed for grouping and logically arranging rules within and across directories significantly influence the clarity, maintainability, and scalability of the build system. This section delineates principles and patterns designed to optimize rule structuring and facilitate incremental growth.

A rule, in the context of build systems, ties together targets, dependencies, and commands that transform inputs into outputs. The declarative specification should be explicit, minimizing implicit assumptions to reduce the cognitive load on maintainers. Rules must exhibit the following characteristics:

- **Atomicity**: Each rule performs a clear, distinct operation, whether it is compilation, linking, or packaging.

- **Determinism**: Rule declarations consistently reflect deterministic output based on given inputs without side effects.

- **Reusability**: Repetitive patterns should be abstracted into reusable macros or templates to avoid duplication.

- **Explicit Dependencies**: All necessary input files and prerequisites must be enumerated to ensure correct incremental builds.

Adherence to these principles facilitates robust dependency tracking, predictable build outcomes, and ease of debugging.

When organizing rules within a single directory, grouping by functional or logical roles is advised. This often corresponds to source code modules, feature sets, or compilation stages. Common effective groupings include:

- **Source-to-Object Compilation Rules**: Rules that transform source files (`.c`, `.cpp`, `.java`) into compiled object files or class files.

- **Library or Archive Creation Rules**: Aggregation of objects into intermediate static or dynamic libraries.

- **Linking Rules**: Linking object files and libraries to produce final executables or shared objects.

- **Testing and Verification Rules**: Invocation of test runners, static analysis tools, or code coverage instrumentation.

- **Packaging and Deployment Rules**: Procedures that assemble distribution artifacts, such as compressed archives or installation packages.

Each group should be visually separated in the build script-often by whitespace or comments-and further modularized via internal

44

macros or functions. For example, macros to compile different types of source files reduce clutter and signal intent clearly.

For larger projects, rules are naturally distributed across multiple directories. The build system must navigate this hierarchy coherently, leveraging directory-level encapsulation while preserving global coherence.

Two prominent strategies prevail:

Hierarchical Delegation

Each directory contains a build script defining local rules for its contents, typically culminating in an aggregation target (e.g., a local library). Higher-level directories then depend upon these aggregation targets, recursively building more complex artifacts. This pattern mirrors the project's source tree structure and fosters locality of change. When a subdirectory changes internally, only that component rebuilds, limiting unnecessary global rebuilds.

Centralized Control with Modular Inclusions

Alternatively, a centralized build script may include or import multiple smaller scripts residing in subdirectories as modules. These modules export their rule sets or targets, which the central script then composes into higher-level targets. This consolidates configuration but demands meticulous namespace management to prevent conflicts. Modularization techniques such as prefixing or scoped variables often accompany this approach.

Pattern 1: Descriptive Naming Conventions

Adopt a naming scheme for rules and targets that encodes their purpose and scope. For example, prefixing with the directory or module name-for instance, `net_compile`, `ui_test`-improves readability and reduces collisions in global namespaces.

Pattern 2: Parameterized Rule Macros

Define parameterized macros or functions to encapsulate common rule structures. This reduces boilerplate, encourages consistency, and simplifies adjustments. For instance:

```
define compile_source(source, target)
  $(CC) -c $(source) -o $(target)
endef
```

Usage of this macro across directories guarantees uniform compilation flags and error handling.

Pattern 3: Layered Dependency Graphs

Organize targets in dependency layers to maintain acyclic build graphs. Base layers compile raw sources, middle layers create libraries, and top layers build executables or packages. Strict layering prevents circular dependencies and simplifies incremental builds.

Pattern 4: Separation of Interface and Implementation

In multi-directory projects, maintain clear boundaries between interface and implementation targets. Interface directories export headers or API stubs without containing implementation details. Build rules reflect this separation, facilitating parallel development and modular rebuilds.

As rule sets expand, scalability challenges arise from increased rule count, intricate dependencies, and diverse build variants (e.g., debug vs. release).

To mitigate these:

- Implement **Caching and Reuse** for rule definitions shared across directories to avoid redundant parsing and evaluation.

- Employ **Conditional Inclusion** of rules tailored to build variants, enabling a lean rule set per build configuration.

- Utilize **Meta-Rules** that generate sets of related rules programmatically based on directory contents or configuration files, reducing manual maintenance.

- Enforce **Consistent Abstraction Layers**, preventing low-level rules from leaking upward and increasing coupling.

Automation via scripting or build system extensions often complements these techniques, dynamically generating or validating rule
declarations.

The above strategies combine to form a robust methodology for
declaring and organizing build rules. By explicitly grouping related
rules, defining clear naming conventions and hierarchies, and abstracting repetitive logic, maintainers can construct scalable and
understandable build configurations. The discipline applied in
rule organization directly influences build performance, ease of
troubleshooting, and agility in responding to evolving project requirements.

2.4. Macros for Reusability

Macros serve as a fundamental abstraction mechanism to encapsulate repetitive build logic within complex build systems. Their
primary function is to enhance maintainability and consistency by
centralizing repeated patterns of code, thereby reducing duplication across multiple BUILD files. In modern build environments,
macros enable layered composition, safe parameterization, and
modular extensibility, all essential for handling the increasing complexity of software projects.

A macro is essentially a user-defined function that generates build
rules or targets based on input parameters. Unlike raw rule instan-
tiations, defining a macro allows developers to abstract away low-
level details, presenting a simplified interface tailored to common
patterns. This abstraction not only streamlines the build files but
also facilitates changes in build logic through single-point updates
instead of widespread edits.

Macro authoring begins with identifying recurring patterns in
build definitions. For example, consider a project that frequently

47

compiles C++ libraries with similar compiler flags and dependencies. Instead of repeating the `cc_library` rule numerous times with identical parameters, a macro can encapsulate the pattern:

```
def cpp_library_macro(name, srcs, deps=[], hdrs=[], copts=[]):
    cc_library(
        name = name,
        srcs = srcs,
        hdrs = hdrs,
        deps = deps,
        copts = copts + ["-Wall", "-Werror"]
    )
```

This macro, `cpp_library_macro`, abstracts the addition of compiler options -Wall and -Werror, which would otherwise be repeated. It takes explicit parameters allowing the caller to customize sources, dependencies, headers, and compiler options while guaranteeing a baseline configuration.

Key considerations in macro authoring include:

- **Parameter Selection**: Macros should expose only the necessary parameters, avoiding unnecessary complexity while retaining flexibility.

- **Defaults and Overrides**: Providing sensible default values ensures convenience; callers can override them when project-specific customization is needed.

- **Type Consistency**: Parameters must have expected types and value constraints to prevent incorrect usage or build errors.

Layering macros is an effective technique to build modular and composable build logic. Lower-level macros encapsulate generic behavior, while higher-level macros specialize or augment that functionality for domain-specific needs.

For instance, a base macro may define generic Java library rules:

```
def java_library_base(name, srcs, deps=[], visibility=[]):
```

```
java_library(
    name = name,
    srcs = srcs,
    deps = deps,
    visibility = visibility
)
```

A higher-level macro can then extend it to enforce usage conventions, such as adding annotation processors or default dependencies:

```
def java_library_with_annotation(name, srcs, deps=[],
    annotation_processors=[]):
    java_library_base(
        name = name,
        srcs = srcs,
        deps = deps + annotation_processors
    )
```

This layering pattern facilitates code reuse and isolates changes: modifications in the base macro propagate through dependent macros transparently. Furthermore, it enables teams to expose simplified, opinionated interfaces suited to specific contexts without duplicating underlying logic.

Macros must accept parameters safely to avoid subtle errors during build execution. Because parameters flow directly into rule definitions, improper handling can lead to cryptic failures or unintentional side effects.

Parameter safety involves several practices:

- **Explicit Types and Mutability**: Parameters should use immutable data types such as tuples or lists consistently. Passing mutable or ambiguous types may cause unexpected behavior.

- **Input Validation**: Macros can include conditional checks to validate parameters and raise errors early. For example, enforcing non-empty source lists:

```
if not srcs:
```

```
fail("Parameter 'srcs' must contain at least one source file
")
```

- **Avoiding Side Effects**: Macros should refrain from modifying arguments in-place. Instead, they should create copies or combine inputs safely to prevent influencing caller state.

- **Encoding Semantic Constraints**: When certain parameters impose semantic requirements (e.g., source files must have specific extensions), macros may include assertions or utility functions to enforce compliance.

Proper parameter validation and sanitization minimize debugging efforts by catching errors near the source rather than during rule execution.

By factoring common patterns into macros, build files become declarative, concise, and focused on intent rather than boilerplate. Consider the alternative: repeating detailed, verbose build rules in dozens of places. Code duplication not only complicates maintenance but also increases the risk of inconsistencies and divergence as projects evolve.

Macros complement other build system features such as load statements and configuration flags, but their role in eliminating duplication is distinctive because they operate at the semantic level of build rule generation. When macros encompass cross-cutting build logic-such as enforcing company-wide settings, integrating toolchains, or standardizing test configurations-they become critical to maintaining uniformity at scale.

One notable pattern is centralizing macro definitions into shared repositories or files imported across multiple downstream packages. This decouples macro logic from individual build files and encourages reuse and collaboration. Furthermore, versioning these macro libraries enables controlled evolution without breaking existing builds.

- Maintain clear and consistent naming conventions, reflecting purpose and granularity.

- Document macros thoroughly, describing parameters, variants, and expected behavior to ease adoption.

- Design macros to be composable, minimizing assumptions and dependencies on global state.

- Utilize layering to isolate generic from specialized concerns, enhancing maintainability.

- Implement comprehensive input validation to prevent misuse and ambiguous errors.

- Test macros independently where possible, verifying correct rule generation and parameter handling.

Adhering to these principles transforms macros from simple conveniences into powerful instruments for scalable build management.

To illustrate, a parameterized macro for constructing Python binaries may abstract environment configuration and dependency injection:

```
def python_binary_macro(name, srcs, main_py, deps=[],
    python_version="3.8"):
    py_binary(
        name = name,
        srcs = srcs,
        main = main_py,
        deps = deps,
        python_version = python_version
    )
```

This macro reduces redundancy by embedding the common version configuration and centralizing binary setup logic. Callers simply specify their sources, main entry point, and dependencies. If the project later requires upgrading the Python version, changing the default in the macro suffices to propagate the update globally.

Macros, when designed and applied conscientiously, provide an abstraction layer that promotes code reuse, enforces consistency,

51

and mitigates duplication across BUILD files. The techniques of authoring, layering, and safe parameterization converge to yield a scalable, maintainable build architecture capable of evolving alongside complex codebases.

2.5. Visibility, Aliasing, and Packaging

Control over target accessibility and encapsulation is foundational to maintainable and scalable software architectures, particularly within large repositories housing complex interdependent components. Visibility attributes, aliasing mechanisms, and packaging strategies collectively enable precise management of symbol scope, modularity, and API exposure. This section explores these advanced techniques to guide developers in structuring and safeguarding large codebases.

Visibility attributes dictate the accessibility of targets—functions, variables, classes, or other symbols—across translation units and linked binaries. They serve as a primary tool in enforcing encapsulation at the binary and compiler levels.

Modern toolchains provide several kinds of visibility controls, commonly categorized as *default, hidden, protected,* and *internal.* The default visibility allows full symbol exportation accessible by all dependent binaries. Hidden visibility restricts symbol exposure to the defining shared object or static library, ensuring internal symbols are not visible outside the compilation unit, thereby reducing symbol collisions and improving load-time efficiency. Protected visibility allows external references but prohibits interposition, preserving symbol semantics while preventing overrides.

Explicit annotation of symbols typically requires compiler-specific attributes. For instance, in GCC and Clang:

```
__attribute__((visibility("hidden"))) void helper_function();
__attribute__((visibility("default"))) void public_api_function()
  ;
```

On Windows platforms, analogous control is exerted via `__declspec(dllexport)` and `__declspec(dllimport)` to manage dynamic-link library symbol visibility, which must be carefully synchronized across compilation units using macros.

Control of visibility influences linking behavior significantly. By minimizing externally visible symbols, linkers can optimize symbol resolution time and reduce potential conflicts during load or runtime. Moreover, visibility governs symbol binding, affecting dynamic linking and the use of techniques such as symbol interposition in shared libraries.

Aliasing plays a crucial role in managing large codebases by providing alternative names for targets, facilitating backward compatibility, namespace management, and conditional exposure of functionality. Aliases allow the introduction of polymorphic behaviors, versioning abstractions, or adaptation layers without redundant duplication.

In C and C++, aliases can be created at the symbol level using compiler directives or linker scripts. GCC provides the `alias` attribute to assign an alternative name to an existing function or variable:

```
void original_function();
void alias_function() __attribute__((alias("original_function")))
    ;
```

This directs the linker to treat `alias_function` as an alias to `original_function`, saving code space and ensuring identical behavior under both names.

Aliasing mechanisms extend beyond simple name equivalences. In build systems that support target-level aliasing, such as CMake, logical target aliases allow grouping or substituting targets without changing their underlying implementation, enabling flexible dependency specifications:

```
add_library(core_lib STATIC core.cpp)
add_library(core_alias ALIAS core_lib)
```

53

Here, `core_alias` becomes a transparent alias for `core_lib`, so downstream targets can depend on `core_alias` to abstract away implementation details or to handle multiple versions.

In large repositories with cross-platform or layered architectures, aliasing facilitates migration paths by allowing newer implementations to shadow older targets while maintaining compatibility through persistent aliases. This approach reduces refactoring costs and supports gradual modernization.

Effective packaging strategies define the structure and accessibility of components, arranging them into coherent units—libraries, modules, or namespaces—that encapsulate internal details while exposing carefully curated APIs.

Logical packaging involves the semantic grouping of related functionality into namespaces or modules, improving code readability and discoverability. Physical packaging pertains to the organization of source files, build targets, and binary artifacts, influencing linkage, dependency resolution, and distribution.

In large monorepos, a hierarchy of packages segmented by functionality and stability is common. Packages with stable, public APIs serve as foundations, while experimental or internal packages remain isolated to reduce risk of unintended dependencies.

Granular control over API exposure enforces encapsulation within packages. Typical strategies include:

- **Header Visibility Control:** Organizing public headers separately from private ones and configuring build systems to install only the public subset. This guarantees that internal implementation headers remain inaccessible to external consumers.

- **Symbol Visibility Management:** As detailed earlier, controlling symbol exportation through compiler attributes or linker scripts complements header separation to prevent inadvertent exposure.

- **Modularization:** Emerging language features and build systems support explicit module boundaries, encapsulating implementation details more robustly than traditional header-based inclusion.

Within large repositories, APIs evolve continuously. Maintaining backward compatibility while introducing new functionality demands explicit API versioning schemes:

- **Symbol Versioning:** Linkers can associate version tags with exported symbols, allowing multiple versions of the same symbol to coexist and clients to bind to desired versions.

- **Namespace or Prefixing Conventions:** Logical segregation of API versions via namespaces or symbol prefixes prevents conflicts and clarifies compatibility guarantees.

- **Deprecation Policies:** Systematic marking of obsolete APIs with clear migration paths encourages gradual adaptation without compromising existing consumers.

Effective packaging requires careful build system design to automate visibility enforcement, alias generation, and API exposure. Tools like CMake, Bazel, or custom build orchestrations provide commands to define target properties, visibility scopes, and alias relationships.

A representative CMake snippet illustrates controlled API exposure and aliasing:

```
add_library(core_lib SHARED core.cpp)
target_include_directories(core_lib
  PUBLIC
    $<BUILD_INTERFACE:${CMAKE_CURRENT_SOURCE_DIR}/include>
    $<INSTALL_INTERFACE:include>)
set_target_properties(core_lib PROPERTIES
```

```
  VERSION 1.2.3
  SOVERSION 1)
add_library(core_alias ALIAS core_lib)
install(TARGETS core_lib EXPORT coreTargets
  LIBRARY DESTINATION lib
  ARCHIVE DESTINATION lib
  RUNTIME DESTINATION bin)
install(DIRECTORY include/ DESTINATION include)
```

This example defines a shared library with specified versioning and visibility, installs headers and binaries into appropriate directories, and creates an alias for flexible referencing.

Overall, visibility attributes minimize accidental symbol exposure, enhancing encapsulation and reducing binary-level dependencies. Aliasing mechanisms establish flexible naming and versioning schemes without code duplication. Packaging strategies—through logical grouping, API granularity, and build system enforcement— safeguard internal implementations while providing stable, well-defined interfaces for large-scale projects. Mastery of these mechanisms is imperative for engineering robust, maintainable software systems in complex environments.

2.6. Maintaining Large-scale Build Definitions

The maintenance of large-scale build definitions, particularly those expressed in BUILD and WORKSPACE files, requires a disciplined architectural approach to ensure long-term scalability, readability, and robustness. As projects grow, ad hoc additions and patching practices inevitably lead to an erosion of clarity and increased fragility. The following architectural best practices address this challenge through modularization, systematic refactoring, rigorous code review, comprehensive documentation, and the integration of automated tooling, thus preserving the integrity and agility of build systems.

Central to scaling BUILD definitions is **modularization**. Instead of aggregating a monolithic BUILD file per repository or even per directory tree, dividing build definitions into focused, reusable modules promotes separation of concerns and reduces interdependency complexity. Each module should encapsulate logically cohesive targets, often aligned with a functional or library boundary in the source code. This modularization facilitates parallel development, reduces cognitive load on engineers, and enables incremental updates with minimal risk. A practical technique is to define *common build macros* and *repository rules* in separate Starlark files imported into BUILD files as needed. This promotes DRY (Don't Repeat Yourself) principles by abstracting repetitive patterns or intricate configurations behind parametrized functions, avoiding duplication and easing propagation of improvements.

Code review plays a critical role in maintaining build definitions at scale. Build files represent a domain-specific language that interacts deeply with the project's source layout, dependency graph, and toolchain constraints. Reviewers must validate not only syntax correctness but also architectural consistency and performance implications such as avoiding unnecessary transitive dependencies or redundant target definitions. Establishing strict review guidelines for build changes helps enforce modularization rules, encourages thoughtful naming conventions, and prevents the unchecked proliferation of sprawling targets. Including build engineers or team members familiar with the build system's internals in the review process drastically improves quality and reduces integration risks.

Complementing code review is the imperative for **comprehensive documentation**. Large-scale build systems are often the result of years of accumulated knowledge, and undocumented changes rapidly degrade maintainability. Each BUILD or WORKSPACE file, or module of build macros, should contain clear comments describing the purpose, scope, and any architectural assumptions. In addition, maintaining centralized documentation that overviews the build system's structure, usage guidelines, and refactoring patterns accelerates onboarding and reduces errors. Inline comments should highlight rationale behind complex rules, any custom patches or third-party dependencies, and deprecation statuses. Employing markup compatible with documentation tools can integrate these insights into autogenerated system reports or developer portals, ensuring coherence across the development ecosystem.

Automated tooling is indispensable for confident refactoring and scaling of build systems. First, **linting and static analysis** tools, custom-tailored to the build language, can identify anti-patterns, deprecated usage, or violations of architectural guidelines. Rule sets can enforce modularization boundaries, naming conventions, or disallow certain patterns such as excessive globbing that hinders incremental builds. Second, **automated formatting** tools ensure uniform style across build files, reducing review overhead and merge conflicts. Third, **build graph analysis tools** visualize dependencies and detect cycles or overly large dependency closures, guiding refactoring efforts and revealing hidden coupling. Fourth, **automated testing frameworks** validate that changes to build definitions do not break reproducibility or cause unintended side effects by running hermetic builds and end-to-end integration tests. Together, such tooling empowers engineers to act with greater confidence and velocity in evolving complex build configurations.

Handling large-scale refactors demands strategic processes and tooling support. When decomposing monolithic BUILD files or reorganizing workspace definitions, incremental steps minimize disruption. One approach involves introducing new modularized build files in parallel to legacy constructs and gradually transitioning consumer targets through aliases or deprecations. This staged migration ensures existing build invocations succeed during refactoring and reduces risk. Advanced use of Starlark macros abstracts low-level configuration details, allowing large-scale changes to be applied by modifying macro implementations rather than individual targets. Automated scripts that propagate changes or rename targets systematically help align files with architectural refreshes. Version control tools with powerful rename and move tracking facilitate migration visibility and conflict resolution.

The following excerpt demonstrates a modularized pattern leveraging Starlark macros to encapsulate a common test target configuration, abstracting complexity and enhancing maintainability:

```
# In //build_rules/test_rules.bzl
def common_test(name, srcs, deps):
    native.cc_test(
        name = name,
        srcs = srcs,
        deps = deps,
        copts = ["-Wall", "-Werror"],
        size = "small",
        tags = ["manual"],
    )

# In a BUILD file
load("//build_rules:test_rules.bzl", "common_test")

common_test(
    name = "fast_math_tests",
    srcs = ["fast_math_tests.cc"],
    deps = [
        "//libs/math:fast_math",
        "//third_party/gtest",
    ],
)
```

This approach concentrates shared configuration details in a single location, enabling holistic updates across all test targets by editing `common_test`. Additionally, it reduces redundancy in BUILD files, improving readability and decreasing the potential for configuration drift.

Ultimately, maintaining large-scale BUILD and WORKSPACE files demands a balanced combination of architectural design, disciplined collaboration, and continuous integration of automation. Modularization partitions complexity, code reviews enforce quality and architectural coherence, documentation preserves institutional knowledge, and tooling enables safe, consistent evolution. These principles collectively transform build system maintenance from a reactive chore into a structured engineering practice, scalable to the largest codebases and evolving as first-class project infrastructure.

Chapter 3

Starlark: Extending Bazel

Ever wished your build system bent to your project instead of the other way around? With Starlark—the expressive, hermetic extension language designed for Bazel—you gain the power to codify custom rules, inject business logic, and automate the impossible. This chapter unlocks the art and science of extending Bazel, walking you from Starlark fundamentals to advanced patterns that let you transform Bazel into your own purpose-built build machine.

3.1. Starlark Language Fundamentals

Starlark is a deterministic, hermetic language designed primarily for configuration and extension in large-scale build systems. Its syntax and semantics draw heavily from Python, ensuring ease of adoption for Python programmers while imposing constraints that promote reproducibility and security within hermetic execution environments. This section delineates the core syntax, data types, and semantic principles of Starlark, emphasizing its distinctions from Python and the implications of its hermetic execution model.

Starlark inherits a Python-like indentation-based block structure, avoiding braces or explicit delimiters for code blocks. Each statement ideally resides on a separate line, and code is organized into sequences of statements and expressions.

Comments begin with # and continue to the line's end, identical to Python. However, unlike Python, Starlark does not support multi-line string literals used as docstrings or embedded comments. String literals may be enclosed in single or double quotes, supporting only single-line strings without escape sequences for multi-line continuation.

Control flow structures include if-else, for, and while statements. Unlike Python, the while loop is rarely used within typical Starlark code due to deterministic behavior constraints. The for loop iterates over sequences and supports break and continue statements, similar to Python.

Function definitions use the def keyword, supporting positional and keyword arguments but disallowing variable-length argument lists (no *args or **kwargs) and default mutable arguments, ensuring function purity and determinism.

```
def factorial(n):
    if n < 2:
        return 1
    prod = 1
    i = 2
    while i <= n:
        prod = prod * i
        i = i + 1
    return prod
```

Starlark's type system distinguishes explicitly between immutable and mutable types, emphasizing constructs that maintain determinism.

Immutable types:

62

- `int` — arbitrary precision integers without overflow, essential for safe arithmetic.

- `bool` — Boolean values `True` and `False`.

- `string` — UTF-8 encoded text, immutable by definition.

- `tuple` — immutable ordered sequences of heterogeneous elements.

- `None` — a singleton representing absence of value.

Mutable types include:

- `list` — mutable sequences with order preserved; appending and modifying elements is allowed.

- `dict` — mutable mappings from immutable keys to arbitrary Starlark values.

Sets are not available as a built-in data type in Starlark, diverging from Python.

Key differences from Python include the absence of floating-point numbers-only integer arithmetic is supported to maintain determinism. Additionally, Starlark forbids hashable mutable objects as dictionary keys; only immutable types are acceptable keys, reflecting stricter constraints to avoid non-determinism.

```
x = 42            # int
y = "hello"       # string
flag = True       # bool
lst = [1, 2, 3]   # list
tup = (4, 5)      # tuple
d = {"a": 1, "b": 2}  # dict
```

Expressions in Starlark support arithmetic, comparison, and logical operators, with semantics largely paralleling Python but constrained to preserve hermeticity. Supported arithmetic operators include +, -, *, // (integer division), and % (modulus).

Floating-point and bitwise operators are disallowed to prevent non-deterministic behavior arising from platform-specific representations.

Logical operators and, or, and not operate on boolean values, adhering to short-circuit evaluation. Comparison operators encompass ==, !=, <, <=, >, and >=.

Importantly, the language enforces expressions to be side-effect free whenever possible, confining state modification to explicit statements.

Starlark's execution model is deterministic and hermetic by design. Programs executing under Starlark adhere to strict rules:

- No access to external state beyond explicitly provided inputs. This precludes filesystem, network, or environment variable access during execution.

- All built-in functions and operations are pure, free from side effects and non-deterministic data.

- Evaluation order is well-defined and consistent, preventing variation in program outputs across executions.

This hermetic execution ensures that the same inputs will always generate identical program outputs, which is crucial for reproducible builds and reliable configuration.

Unlike Python's general-purpose environment that allows reflection, dynamic code loading, and unrestricted I/O, Starlark restricts or disables these features explicitly. For instance, module imports are static and confined, and reflection mechanisms such as eval() or exec() do not exist.

Memory management is automatic, with the Starlark interpreter employing garbage collection strategies tailored for incremental build systems. However, reflection and runtime code modification are forbidden, guaranteeing program state can be reasoned about completely at definition time.

While Starlark is a dialect inspired by Python, notable differences underscore its specialized purpose:

- **Determinism**: Starlark forbids all non-deterministic constructs. Floating-point arithmetic, system calls, and random number generation are disallowed.

- **Simplified syntax**: Certain Python features such as list comprehensions, lambda functions, and generators are omitted for simplicity and clarity.

- **Restricted built-ins**: Only a minimal set of built-in functions are available, focused on essential computation and data manipulation.

- **No exceptions**: Starlark does not support user-defined exceptions or try-except blocks; runtime errors terminate execution immediately.

- **Immutable hashing keys**: Dictionary keys must be immutable, preventing unexpected mutations that could violate deterministic behaviors.

- **No classes or inheritance**: Object-oriented features are absent to maintain simplicity and predictability.

These restrictions enable Starlark to serve as a robust platform for configuration and extension authoring within build systems, balancing expressiveness with the demands of performance and reproducibility.

The fundamental semantic principles ensuring Starlark's utility in hermetic build environments can be summarized as follows:

- **Immutability where possible**: Immutable data structures and pure functions are favored.

65

- **Deterministic computation**: All operations produce identical outputs for identical inputs, independent of external factors.

- **Controlled side effects**: Mutable state and side effects are tightly scoped and explicit.

- **No interaction with the host environment**: Execution is sandboxed from system resources.

These principles underlie the language's role as a predictable, extensible configuration mechanism suitable for large-scale, distributed systems where repeatability and safety are paramount.

3.2. Defining Custom Build Rules

Custom build rules in Bazel, authored with Starlark, form the nucleus of tailored build logic, allowing precise control over how inputs are transformed into outputs. A robust, reusable build rule encapsulates behavior in a modular and declarative fashion, exposing fine-grained parameters while managing execution context and lifecycle events with predictability. This section deconstructs the essential components of such rules: their anatomy, the rule context, attribute handling, output declarations, and the sequential lifecycle events necessary for comprehensive custom integrations.

At the core, a build rule in Starlark is a function, typically declared with the `rule()` macro, that describes the parameters and execution logic associated with a build target. The `rule()` function returns a *rule object* which the build system interprets. The backbone of this definition includes: an `implementation` function, an `attrs` dictionary specifying input attributes, and optional elements such as `outputs` declarations and validity predicates.

A minimal custom rule definition has the general form:

```
def _implementation(ctx):
    # Build actions are declared here
    pass

my_rule = rule(
    implementation = _implementation,
    attrs = {
        "srcs": attr.label_list(allow_files=True),
        "deps": attr.label_list(),
        "visibility": attr.visibility(),
    },
    outputs = {"out": "%{name}.out"},
)
```

The _implementation function is the operational heart, receiving a ctx (context) argument representing the rule context. This function must orchestrate build *actions*-commands or artifacts' generation-while abiding by declared inputs, outputs, and declared dependencies. The attrs parameter specifies the input interface for the rule, exposing fully typed attributes from which the implementation derives its behavior. Outputs may be explicitly defined through the outputs dictionary, allowing automated file path templating via label expansions.

The rule context (ctx) abstracts the build environment for a single instance of the rule. It represents the cohesive state encapsulating all information necessary to evaluate dependencies, retrieve attribute values, declare outputs, and register build actions. The context exposes several critical fields and methods:

- ctx.attr: A namespace providing direct access to the rule's attributes, as filtered and validated by Bazel. For example, ctx.attr.srcs gives a list of declared source files or targets.

- ctx.outputs: Provides access to output files for the current target, allowing the implementation function to specify files generated by the rule. For example, ctx.outputs.out refers to the declared output filename corresponding to "out" in the outputs dictionary.

- `ctx.actions`: A factory for actions. This namespace exposes methods such as `ctx.actions.run()`, `ctx.actions.write()`, and `ctx.actions.symlink()` to register build actions with precise command lines, input/output file dependencies, and environment control.

- `ctx.fragments`: Provides low-level access to platform-specific configuration fragments (if any are enabled), enabling integration with build metadata such as toolchain configurations or compilation flags.

Correct understanding and utilization of `ctx` are critical for precise build rule functionality. It ensures output generation guards against undeclared inputs and appropriately propagates dependencies, ensuring build graph correctness.

Attributes define the interface by which a rule interacts with its inputs. The attribute schema must be carefully specified through the `attrs` dictionary, leveraging an extensive attribute API that enforces type safety and offers configurability:

```
attrs = {
    "srcs": attr.label_list(allow_files=True, mandatory=True),
    "deps": attr.label_list(cfg="target", providers=[MyInfo]),
    "flag": attr.string(default="--opt"),
    "visibility": attr.visibility(),
}
```

Key attribute types include:

- `attr.label`: Single dependency reference to a target.

- `attr.label_list`: Multiple dependency targets.

- `attr.string`, `attr.int`, `attr.bool`: Primitive user-supplied parameters.

- `attr.files`: File collections.

Attributes support additional parameters controlling configuration transitions (e.g., `cfg`), allowable file types, mandatory require-

68

ments, default values, and more. Attributes not explicitly declared remain inaccessible within `ctx.attr`, ensuring strict attribute contract enforcement.

Explicit output declaration plays a vital role in modern Bazel workflows by clarifying generated artifacts, enabling incremental builds, content-addressable caching, and hermeticity. Output specifications define named outputs relative to the build target directory, often templated by label components:

```
outputs = {
    "binary": "%{name}.exe",
    "log": "%{name}.log",
}
```

Within the implementation, these outputs become accessible via `ctx.outputs.binary` or `ctx.outputs.log`. Declaring outputs explicitly avoids side-effect generation, improving reproducibility and enabling Bazel to track artifact dependencies with precision.

For more complex output naming logic, the `ctx.actions.declare_file()` method allows dynamic file declaration based on the rule's inputs or logic paths, though this negates some tooling conveniences.

Rule implementations execute in a deterministic lifecycle: attribute evaluation, output declaration, and action registration. Actions represent atomic steps executed during the build, and must be precisely declared with input and output file parameters. Actions can be shell commands, writing files, or signaling file system operations.

```
ctx.actions.run(
    inputs = ctx.attr.srcs,
    outputs = [ctx.outputs.binary],
    executable = "/usr/bin/gcc",
    arguments = ctx.attr.srcs + ["-o", ctx.outputs.binary.path],
    mnemonic = "CompileBinary",
    progress_message = "Compiling binary %s" % ctx.label.name,
)
```

The `ctx.actions.run()` method describes a command-line action, specifying:

- `inputs`: Declared input files or targets.

- `outputs`: Files generated by the action.

- `executable`: Absolute or workspace-relative executable path.

- `arguments`: List of command arguments.

- `mnemonic`: Short name useful for logging and profiling.

- `progress_message`: User-friendly progress log message.

Additional actions include `ctx.actions.write()` for generating file contents from strings or binaries, and `ctx.actions.symlink()` for symbolic link creation. Each action must faithfully declare all dependencies to guarantee incremental correctness in dependency tracking.

Attention must be paid to side effects and redundant actions; each build action should be idempotent given identical inputs and produce all declared outputs to maintain Bazel's cache correctness and reproducibility guarantees.

Robust custom rules emphasize clarity, reusability, and parameterization:

- Keep the `implementation` function focused on action declarations, minimizing side effects.

- Rigorously validate and document attributes using the available `attr` types.

- Favor explicit output declarations over dynamic output names for performance benefits.

- Leverage `ctx.actions` API for all effects, avoiding implicit file operations.

- Modularize complex logic into helper Starlark functions to promote reuse.

- Use `mnemonic` and descriptive `progress_messages` to aid debugging and build introspection.

By mastering these facets-defining a precise attribute schema, utilizing the rule context to its full extent, declaring outputs rigorously, and registering deterministic actions-a Starlark author crafts custom build rules that integrate seamlessly into the Bazel ecosystem with predictability, efficiency, and maintainability.

3.3. Starlark Providers and Data Propagation

In build systems based on Starlark, *providers* facilitate structured and type-safe data exchange between rules and macros, establishing a contract for modular and maintainable build logic. Providers encapsulate information produced by a rule, allowing downstream rules to introspect, combine, and act on that data without depending on implementation-specific details. This abstraction enables complex interactions, improves encapsulation, and enhances extensibility.

A provider is fundamentally a Starlark object that carries a well-defined set of fields. Providers are attached as components of a rule's output, commonly embedded in the `DefaultInfo` provider alongside standard artifacts, environment variables, and metadata. However, custom providers extend this mechanism by allowing arbitrary, rule-specific data to propagate through the build graph. By representing provider instances using a declarative schema, Starlark ensures that consumers can safely access expected attributes while enabling compile-time and tooling benefits.

Standard providers function as predefined interfaces representing common build information. For example, `DefaultInfo` provides `files`, `runfiles`, and `env` fields, whereas `FileInfo` represents file metadata. Custom providers are user-defined constructs specified via provider() calls, defining named fields that describe the data exposed by a rule.

```
MyInfo = provider(fields = ["label", "output_files", "metadata"])

def _my_rule_impl(ctx):
    out_files = [ctx.actions.declare_file(ctx.label.name + ".txt
    ")]
    # Action creation omitted for brevity
    return [MyInfo(label = ctx.label, output_files = out_files,
    metadata = {"key": "value"})]

my_rule = rule(
    implementation = _my_rule_impl,
    attrs = {},
)
```

Here, MyInfo is a provider with three fields that describe essential outputs and metadata relevant to its consumer rules.

When a rule consumes other targets, it gains access to their providers through the ctx.attr… attributes, which expose the provider instances declared by dependencies. This mechanism promotes a form of controlled data flow, where rules selectively import data necessary for their processing.

Consider a consumer_rule that depends on my_rule and extracts its MyInfo provider to perform further computation:

```
def _consumer_rule_impl(ctx):
    myinfo = ctx.attr.dep[MyInfo]
    out_label = myinfo.label
    outputs = myinfo.output_files
    meta = myinfo.metadata
    # Utilize retrieved data, e.g. aggregating outputs or
    processing metadata
    return [DefaultInfo(files = depset(outputs))]

consumer_rule = rule(
    implementation = _consumer_rule_impl,
    attrs = {"dep": attr.label()},
)
```

In this example, the consumer extracts the MyInfo instance from its dependency and operates on its structured data fields. This fa-

cilitates modular build behavior, where rules expose precisely the
data intended for reuse, fostering encapsulation and dependency
decoupling.

Providers can be nested or combined to represent complex data
relationships in multi-stage builds. One rule might aggregate
providers from multiple dependencies, re-emitting a synthesized
provider that enriches the build graph with cumulative knowledge.

```
AggregateInfo = provider(fields = ["all_outputs", "metadata_map
    "])

def _aggregator_rule_impl(ctx):
    outputs = []
    metadata_map = {}
    for dep in ctx.attr.deps:
        info = dep[MyInfo]
        outputs.extend(info.output_files)
        metadata_map[info.label] = info.metadata
    return [AggregateInfo(all_outputs = outputs, metadata_map =
    metadata_map)]

aggregator_rule = rule(
    implementation = _aggregator_rule_impl,
    attrs = {"deps": attr.label_list()},
)
```

The `aggregator_rule` gathers all outputs and metadata from
each dependency's `MyInfo`, synthesizing them into a unified
`AggregateInfo` instance. Downstream rules can then consume
`AggregateInfo` to either inspect or further propagate combined
data.

Providers are designed to represent stable, immutable data shaping the build's semantics. Field names should be descriptive
and consistent, while data types must be Starlark-compatible and
preferably simple to facilitate analysis and caching.

It is advisable to minimize excessive nesting and prevent cyclical
dependencies between providers. Such cycles undermine correctness guarantees and can trigger infinite loops in dependency resolution. Providers should also avoid embedding implementation
details such as internal file paths or mutable state.

Documentation alongside provider definitions is crucial to describe the semantics and intended consumers, as tooling often relies on these contracts to enforce correctness and enable advanced visualization or dependency tracking.

Providers enable the decomposition of complex build operations into reusable, composable units. By explicitly modeling data flows, they help maintain clear separation between rules responsible for generating files and those aggregating or transforming them.

This modularity is especially powerful in large-scale build systems, where multiple teams maintain distinct rule sets. Providers serve as formal APIs between rules, fostering collaboration and facilitating incremental migration or extension.

Furthermore, structured data propagation through providers supports advanced features like selective rebuilds, fine-grained caching, and dynamic dependency computation, all critical for improving build performance and correctness.

While providers offer great flexibility, they should not be used as a panacea for all inter-rule communication. Careful design is required to avoid overly complex provider hierarchies that increase cognitive load and maintenance difficulty.

Moreover, the Starlark implementation environment imposes restrictions on provider content: for example, non-Starlark-serializable entities such as raw file handles or external system objects are disallowed. Providers must remain pure data carriers without invoking side effects during construction.

Finally, debugging provider-related issues can be challenging due to their indirect and abstract nature. Incorporating logging and systematic testing of provider contracts is an effective method to mitigate such risks.

Through judicious creation and use of providers, Starlark empowers rule authors to establish robust and extensible build descriptions. Providers act as formalized data bridges, enabling complex yet maintainable interactions across build stages while maintaining a clear separation of concerns indispensable for scalable build system design.

3.4. Macros versus Rules: Proper Use Cases

Within the Bazel ecosystem, the delineation between macros and rules is a fundamental architectural consideration that directly impacts the maintainability, extensibility, and correctness of build configurations. Both constructs serve to encapsulate build logic but differ markedly in their scope, execution model, and intended application. A rigorous understanding of these differences facilitates the design of robust and efficient build extensions that align with Bazel's principles.

At the core, *rules* represent the primitive programmable entities in Bazel. They explicitly define new build actions and their associated input-output relationships within the build graph. Rules are implemented using Starlark functions decorated with the @rule decorator, which receive structured arguments-such as labels, attributes, and toolchain configurations-and produce configured targets that describe the build graph nodes deterministically. The rule implementation prescribes explicit dependency registration, artifact generation, and environment constraints, making them first-class constructs in Bazel's dependency analysis and incremental build system.

In contrast, *macros* are higher-order Starlark functions that operate solely at load or analysis time and do not introduce new action semantics into the build graph. They serve as syntactic abstractions to generate one or more invocations of existing rules programmatically, effectively acting as a convenience layer to reduce boilerplate and enforce consistent configuration across multiple targets. As macros expand during the loading or analysis phase, they do not themselves create configured targets; instead, they instantiate rules (or other macros), thereby shaping the build dependency graph indirectly. Consequently, macros incur no direct impact on Bazel's action execution mechanisms but influence the overall structure and readability of build files.

The decision to implement functionality as a macro or rule should hinge on the nature of the build logic and the intended scope of reuse or customization. The following considerations outline best practices to promote maintainability and minimize technical debt:

- **Use rules when introducing new build semantics or generating artifacts.** Since rules generate configured targets and define explicit build actions, they are the appropriate abstraction for encapsulating novel compilation steps, custom code generators, or packaging mechanisms. By defining a clear interface with well-specified attributes, rules provide robust encapsulation and integrate seamlessly with Bazel's dependency analysis, caching, and remote execution facilities.

- **Reserve macros for configuration and composition of existing rules.** Macros excel in templating common patterns, parameterizing rule invocations, and expressing complex target sets. They are advantageous for decomposing repetitive build file constructs, establishing standard naming conventions, or applying consistent attribute transformations across multiple targets without modifying the build graph semantics.

- **Avoid embedding significant logic or stateful computations inside macros.** Since macros execute at load time, heavy computations can degrade startup performance and complicate debugging. Instead, such logic should be encapsulated within rule implementations or Starlark libraries leveraged by rules. Macros should remain as declarative and side-effect-free as possible.

- **Prefer explicit attributes in rules over implicit configurations via macros.** Building extensible and maintainable rules requires exposing configuration points via well-typed attributes rather than relying on hidden environment assumptions influenced by macros. This improves rule composability and reduces opaque dependencies that can lead to brittle build files.

- **Leverage macros to mediate transition during incremental refactoring.** Macros can temporarily provide backward compatibility wrappers around evolving rule APIs or orchestrate gradual migration paths as rules change. This decoupling prevents monolithic rule changes from propagating instability throughout consuming build files.

- **Document the intended use and invariants of each macro and rule.** Clear documentation helps future maintainers understand the correct extension points and discourages misuse that can result in tangled dependencies or obscure build errors.

A common anti-pattern to avoid is the overuse of macros to simulate rules by embedding complex dependency resolution or generating outputs indirectly. This undermines Bazel's clear separation between build graph definition and graph instantiation, leading to hard-to-debug behavior caused by implicit or volatile build graph mutations. Conversely, implementing all logic as rules can cause unnecessary verbosity in straightforward build configurations better expressed as macros.

The demarcation also affects caching and incremental build correctness. Since rules define the content hashes of their inputs and outputs, their deterministic implementation guarantees correct incremental rebuilds. Macros, by contrast, have no equivalently fine-grained caching, being evaluated eagerly during the load phase; excessive reliance on macros can slow loading and hinder scalability.

To summarize the interplay:

- **Rules** define *what* is built, establishing new build entities and actions.

- **Macros** define *how* these entities are combined or orchestrated, simplifying user-facing build files.

An effective strategy in large-scale Bazel extension development is to adopt a layered approach: implement stable, well-tested primitives as rules with explicit attributes supporting necessary configuration. Then, build on these foundations via macros that tailor usage patterns and aid ergonomic consumption in downstream build files.

In practical terms, a rule implementation might expose parameters such as compiler flags, source files, and dependencies, while a macro collates these into a standardized naming schema, adds default dependencies, or instantiates complex target sets representing multiple build variants. This pattern preserves a composable core while enabling streamlined build file syntax.

Ultimately, judicious use of macros and rules ensures that build configurations remain maintainable, adaptable, and performant. Maintaining this discipline reduces technical debt in Bazel extensions, facilitates collaborative development, and leverages Bazel's powerful incremental and distributed build infrastructure effectively.

3.5. Repository Rules in Starlark

Repository rules in Starlark play a crucial role in automating the process of fetching, configuring, and generating external dependencies during the evaluation of a WORKSPACE file. These rules empower users to declaratively specify how external resources-such as remote archives, version-controlled repositories, or dynamically generated sources-are brought into the build environment. Understanding their underlying mechanics is essential for mastering the extension of the build configuration beyond standard repository declarations.

At their core, repository rules encapsulate the logic that determines how external code or assets become visible and usable within a Bazel build. Unlike typical build rules that operate within the source tree and build graph, repository rules execute during the WORKSPACE loading phase. This early execution allows them to dynamically produce or configure directories that Bazel treats as external repositories, thereby enabling other dependent targets to reference them reliably.

A repository rule is defined in Starlark as a function decorated with @repository_rule, which accepts a fixed set of parameters describing the external repository attributes (for instance, URLs, checksum values, or branch names). When invoked in a WORKSPACE file, Bazel launches a dedicated execution context for the rule. This context facilitates reading remote sources, applying configurations, and materializing files on the local filesystem, typically under Bazel's output base, in a path unique to the repository name.

During execution, repository rules perform several key operations:

- **Fetching Remote Content:** Leveraging Starlark APIs, rules can download files via http_archive, git_repository, or custom-defined network fetch techniques. The fetched content can include compressed archives or bare source trees.

- **Unpacking and Configuration:** Once downloaded, archives are unpacked, and repository rules may generate or modify files-for example, applying patches, templating configurations, or extracting subsets of files.

- **Generating BUILD Files:** Since external repositories are separate from the main build, repository rules often generate corresponding BUILD files. These files describe the targets exposed by the repository, enabling Bazel to integrate external code seamlessly with the main build graph.

- **Caching and Reuse:** Bazel maintains a content-addressed caching mechanism to avoid redundant fetching or extraction, using the rule input parameters and fetched content hashes. This guarantees idempotent and efficient repository provisioning.

One powerful feature of repository rules is their capacity for dynamic repository creation. Rather than relying solely on static URLs or hardcoded sources, repository rules can incorporate logic that adapts repository generation based on configuration values, environment variables, or conditional criteria.

For instance, a repository rule may generate templated source files or BUILD configurations at runtime. This process often involves expanding templates with variable substitution or condition-based content modulation. Such templating is typically implemented using Starlark string manipulation combined with file-write primitives:

```
def _template_repo_rule_impl(ctx):
    content = """
    load("@bazel_tools//tools/build_defs/repo:utils.bzl", "
     read_json")
    package(default_visibility = ["//visibility:public"])
    export_files(["%s"])
    """ % ctx.attr.source_file

    ctx.file("BUILD", content)
    ctx.file(ctx.attr.source_file, ctx.file.read(ctx.attr.
     template_file))
```

Dynamic repository creation also enables parameterized repositories that adjust their contents depending on upstream repository statuses, platform-specific variations, or user-defined overrides. This flexibility further integrates complex external dependencies into Bazel's hermetic model without losing declarative clarity.

Managing remote resources effectively is fundamental for repository rules. Bazel enforces strict isolation and integrity constraints by requiring explicit declarations of expected SHA-256 checksums for fetched archives. This protocol guards against supply-chain attacks and ensures reproducible builds.

Repository rules often employ utility functions to download resources, verify checksums, and stage data systematically:

```
def _download_and_verify(ctx, url, sha256):
    archive_file = ctx.download(url, sha256 = sha256)
    ctx.extract(archive_file)
```

In some cases, repository rules may utilize mirrors or fallback locations to increase availability. Advanced rules may incorporate retry logic, proxy configurations, or version resolution strategies, although such operations must be carefully managed within Starlark's limitations (e.g., no direct threading or asynchronous calls).

Repository rules also accommodate version control systems (VCS) through specialized mechanisms like `git_repository`, which clone a repository at a specified commit or tag. This process interacts with Git command-line tools externally but is abstracted by Bazel for hermeticity.

Within the `WORKSPACE` file, repository rules are instantiated with distinctive repository names. These names become the canonical identifiers for external dependencies, referred to by `@repository_name//package:target` labels throughout the build.

Repository rules can reference one another transitively by invoking repository rule functions during their implementation. This capability allows complex dependency trees to be constructed dynamically, facilitating scenarios such as vendoring indirect dependencies or creating layered overlays.

For example, a repository rule can trigger the instantiation of another repository, passing parameters down the chain:

```
def _parent_repo_rule_impl(ctx):
    ctx.call_repository_rule(
        "child_repo_rule",
        args = {"url": ctx.attr.child_url, "sha256": ctx.attr.
    child_sha256}
    )
```

This coordination necessitates careful design to avoid cyclic dependencies and to maintain reproducibility. Bazel enforces acyclicity in repository declarations, ensuring that external repository graphs can be resolved deterministically.

While repository rules are powerful, some practical constraints govern their usage:

- **Pure Functions with Side Effects:** Repository rule implementations are treated as pure functions from Bazel's perspective, where the same inputs must always produce the same outputs. Side effects are restricted to file system changes within the designated output directory.

- **Limited Starlark Standard Library:** Network operations, subprocess execution, or threading must be funneled through dedicated Bazel APIs, as arbitrary shell interactions are disallowed for correctness.

- **Deterministic Generation:** Generated files and directory structures must be stable across runs to guarantee incremental caching and parallel builds.

Adhering to these principles ensures repository rules contribute to reproducible, hermetic builds, fostering trust in external code integration.

Through the mechanisms outlined above, repository rules in Starlark provide a rich, programmable abstraction layer for automating the acquisition and preparation of dependencies. Their design balances flexibility with stringent reproducibility requirements, enabling complex build environments to integrate diverse and

82

evolving external sources reliably. This capability extends Bazel's declarative model beyond internal source trees, encompassing the full lifecycle of software supply chain management within a unified, scriptable domain.

3.6.   Best Practices for Starlark Performance

Achieving high-performance Starlark code requires careful attention to both the inherent constraints of the language and the runtime environment in which it operates. Common pitfalls often stem from misunderstandings of Starlark's evaluation model, memory management nuances, and the potential for extensions to introduce inefficiencies as they scale. This section delineates key strategies to avoid performance regressions and improve efficiency, focusing on caching mechanisms, memory usage optimization, parallelism opportunities, and proactive regression guarding.

Avoiding Common Efficiency Pitfalls

Starlark's interpreted execution model implies that repeated computations, especially those involving expensive function calls or complex data structure manipulations, can degrade performance significantly. Frequently encountered inefficiencies include:

- **Redundant function invocations:** Invoking pure functions multiple times with identical arguments, rather than reusing cached results.

- **Excessive list and dictionary allocations:** Unnecessary creation or copying of mutable collections within loops or frequently called code paths.

- **Inefficient string manipulations:** Repeated use of concatenation operators on large strings, leading to quadratic time and memory overhead.

83

- **Overuse of recursion:** Although supported, deep or naive recursion can exhaust available stack frames and consume excessive CPU.

Mitigating these issues requires idiomatic use of memoization, leveraging immutable data where suitable, and adopting iteration in place of recursion where possible.

Effective Caching Strategies

Memoization stands out as a fundamental optimization for Starlark extensions. Since functions are stateless and side-effect-free by design, caching their outputs based on argument values maximizes reuse without correctness loss. A common pattern utilizes dictionaries as memo tables indexed by argument tuples:

```
def memoize_example(arg1, arg2):
    if not hasattr(memoize_example, "cache"):
        memoize_example.cache = {}
    key = (arg1, arg2)
    if key not in memoize_example.cache:
        # perform expensive computation
        memoize_example.cache[key] = arg1 * arg2  # placeholder
     computation
    return memoize_example.cache[key]
```

While straightforward, this approach requires careful cache size management to prevent memory bloat. Eviction policies can be implemented at the host application layer if supported. Additionally, memoization should only be applied to deterministic functions that have no side effects, as improper use can cause semantic errors.

Optimizing Memory Usage

Due to Starlark's frequent creation of objects and collections, managing memory footprints is critical. Some practical techniques include:

- **Reuse immutable structures:** Since tuples and strings are immutable, sharing them across computations avoids du-

84

plications.

- **Minimize temporary objects:** Especially inside loops, avoid creating new lists or dictionaries when a single shared one can be updated or cleared.

- **Lazy evaluation:** Deferring computation or object construction until values are strictly needed saves upfront allocation costs.

- **Use native host types when possible:** When binding Go or Java libraries to Starlark, host-native data structures with efficient implementations can greatly reduce overhead.

Memory profiling tools integrated into the extension host environment can help identify hotspots and unnecessary allocations contributing to performance degradation.

Leveraging Parallelism

Starlark's runtime semantics are primarily single-threaded to maintain determinism. However, opportunities to exploit parallelism arise at the host application level when multiple independent Starlark interpreters or evaluation contexts are instantiated. Parallel execution can be safely orchestrated if extensions are designed to avoid shared mutable state. Best practices include:

- **Stateless extension functions:** Design functions to be pure and reentrant, facilitating concurrent executions without synchronization.

- **Batch processing:** Partition input data into independent chunks that can be evaluated concurrently in separate interpreter instances.

- **Offloading computation:** Delegate heavy operations to the host language where native parallelism constructs are available, presenting results back to Starlark.

While parallelism improves throughput, it requires careful coordination and monitoring to avoid contention or deadlocks in shared resources external to Starlark.

Guarding Against Performance Regressions

As Starlark extensions evolve and grow, their performance can degrade subtly due to code complexity, feature additions, or changes in data volume. Effective methods to anticipate and detect regressions include:

- **Benchmarking:** Establish microbenchmarks for critical functions and measure key metrics such as execution time and memory consumption per commit or release cycle.

- **Profiling:** Utilize integrated profiling tools to analyze CPU hotspots and object allocations within the Starlark interpreter.

- **Regression tests with performance budgets:** Implement testing frameworks that not only verify correctness but also enforce upper bounds on resource usage.

- **Code reviews with performance focus:** Incorporate performance considerations explicitly in code review criteria to detect costly coding patterns early.

Automation of these practices ensures sustained performance and provides early warnings when modifications introduce latent inefficiencies.

Best Practice Highlights for Starlark Performance

- Cache pure function results explicitly to avoid redundant work.

- Minimize temporary object and collection creations, particularly in hot loops.

- Favor immutable data sharing and lazy computations to reduce memory usage.

- Use the host language's parallel execution capabilities by isolating Starlark interpreter instances.

- Establish benchmarks, profiling, and regression tests to maintain performance during development.

Adhering to these principles ensures that Starlark extensions not only maintain correctness and clarity but also scale gracefully to demanding workloads with reliable and efficient execution.

3.7. Testing and Debugging Starlark Extensions

Testing and debugging are essential components in the lifecycle of developing robust Starlark extensions, particularly given the increasing complexity of build logic and its interactions with the broader build system. The intrinsically declarative and functional style of Starlark scripts demands specialized strategies for verification, simulation, and error diagnosis. This section articulates key methodologies and tooling available to ensure correctness, facilitate isolation during development, and enable effective diagnosis of intricate behaviors in Starlark-driven builds.

Unit testing in Starlark involves isolating discrete functions or modules within the extension to verify their behavior under controlled input scenarios. Given that Starlark itself does not include a built-in testing framework, extensions leverage external harnesses or the testing infrastructure provided by the embedding environment (e.g., Bazel's `starlark_test` rule). The cardinal approach is to structure Starlark code into pure functions or rule implementations with deterministic outputs from defined inputs, facilitating reproducibility.

A typical unit test framework within Bazel consists of:

- A dedicated `starlark_test` target that loads and exercises specific functions or rules.

- Use of assert-like helper functions within Starlark to validate returned data structures or strings.

- Parametrization of test inputs to cover boundary cases, erroneous inputs, and valid scenarios.

An example minimal unit test for a Starlark function computing a transformed label might be written as follows:

```
def test_transform_label():
    input_label = "//foo:bar"
    expected_output = "//foo:baz"
    result = transform_label(input_label)
    assert result == expected_output, "Label transformation
     failed"
```

Validation relies on these assertions triggering test failures if expectations are unmet. To extend coverage, tests often mock external dependencies or inputs.

Complex build logic frequently depends on repository state or indirect interactions with the filesystem and external tools. Since Starlark operates in a restricted sandbox, direct side-effect verification is limited. To approach this, mock environments are employed by simulating external APIs and abstracting over configurable dependencies.

Strategies include:

- Injecting mock target dependencies, such as dummy `File` or `Label` objects, programmed with minimal interfaces just sufficient for testing.

- Overriding global repository attributes or Starlark built-ins in the test environment by supplying alternate implementations.

- Utilizing layered load() directives to interpose mocks over normal rule implementations.

These techniques enable testing sophisticated workflows where the extension under test operates on a simulated DAG of targets or provides a stubbed command execution environment. By controlling these mock inputs precisely, unexpected side effects and race conditions can be better understood before deployment.

Debugging Starlark code is complicated by its execution within a sandboxed interpreter and by the limited runtime introspection primitives available. However, several effective debugging patterns and tools exist:

- **Print Statements:** The simplest and most widespread method. Starlark supports a print() function whose output is captured by the build system and can be viewed in the build logs.

- **Verbose Mode:** Many build systems offer a verbose or debug output flag, increasing the granularity of logged data. This includes detailed traces of rule execution and attribute evaluations.

- **Error Messaging:** Carefully crafted error messages with interpolation of variable states at failure points assist in root-cause identification.

- **Incremental Development:** Building smaller independent rules and testing frequently reduces debugging scope.

Print-based debugging within Starlark might look like:

```
print("Evaluating label:", input_label)
if input_label == "":
    fail("Empty label string")
```

Tracing symbolic execution or stack traces for Starlark failures involves analyzing the error output produced by the build system, which typically includes call stack frames referencing Starlark files and line numbers.

Build extensions increasingly participate within complex graphs of dependencies and conditional logic spanning multiple loaded files. Tracing such interactions requires a multi-faceted approach:

- **Dependency Graph Visualization**: Generating or leveraging existing tools to visualize the target and attribute dependency graph aids understanding of build execution order and side effects.

- **Log Aggregation**: Collecting and filtering logs from multiple sources, including submodules and external repositories, to correlate events during the build.

- **Incremental Execution**: Running partial builds or individual targets to isolate the propagation of errors or unexpected behavior.

Analyzing complex runtime behavior commonly involves iterative refinement of test cases in the mock environment and selective expansion of print-based tracing. Additionally, some build systems provide experimental debuggers or REPLs with limited support for inspecting live Starlark execution.

The effectiveness of testing and debugging in Starlark extensions improves significantly through adherence to a few key principles:

- Maintain strict modularity and purity in function design to simplify unit testing.

- Employ mock objects and configurable inputs to emulate external dependencies.

- Leverage verbose logs and structured print statements for runtime insight.

- Gradually expand testing scope from function-level to entire build rule suites.

- Exploit build system hooks, where available, to capture detailed error reports and execution traces.

By integrating these methodologies, developers can systematically construct, verify, and refine Starlark extensions with high confidence while minimizing troubleshooting time during complex build interactions.

Chapter 4

Advanced Build and Dependency Management

Once your codebase grows beyond a few modules, builds and dependencies become a labyrinth. This chapter guides you through Bazel's most powerful tools and patterns for navigating complex dependency graphs, managing vast webs of transitive relationships, and enforcing reproducible, scalable builds—even in the face of polyglot codebases and external integrations. Here's how leading teams keep Bazel builds fast, clean, and correct at any scale.

4.1. Dependency Graph Analysis and Querying

Bazel's core strength lies in its robust handling of dependencies, enabling incremental builds that are both efficient and correct. The accurate representation and manipulation of the build dependency graph is crucial for understanding project structure, diagnosing build failures, and identifying optimization opportunities. Bazel provides advanced query tools that expose the full dependency graph and allow developers to extract precise, actionable insights from it. These tools facilitate visualization, impact analysis, dead code detection, and build optimization.

The fundamental query command is `bazel query`, which accepts a range of expressions to traverse and filter the build dependency graph. The dependency graph is a directed acyclic graph (DAG) where nodes correspond to build targets, and edges represent dependencies. Queries can analyze both direct and transitive dependencies, expressed as `deps()` for downstream and `rdeps()` for upstream dependencies. For example, to obtain the full transitive closure of dependencies of a target `//app:binary`, the command is:

```
bazel query "deps(//app:binary)"
```

Visualizing this dependency graph helps elucidate the complex relationships between targets. By combining `bazel query` with graph generation tools, the graph can be rendered using Graphviz. For example:

```
bazel query "deps(//app:binary)" --output graph > deps.dot
dot -Tpng deps.dot -o deps.png
```

The output image `deps.png` visualizes nodes and edges, enabling structural analysis. Filtering nodes or edges with additional predicates (such as filtering for rules of a particular kind or paths within certain packages) helps focus on relevant portions.

Impact Analysis

When modifying a target or source file, determining the impact on the overall build and test suite is critical for efficient iteration. Bazel's `rdeps()` operator facilitates impact analysis by identifying all targets that depend (directly or transitively) on a given target, thereby revealing the subset of the build potentially affected by a change.

For instance, to find all test targets that would need to be re-executed after a change in //lib:core, one can run:

```
bazel query "rdeps(//..., //lib:core) intersect kind(test, //...)
    "
```

This query retrieves all test targets in the workspace transitively depending on //lib:core. Limiting queries to specific subsets of the workspace, such as certain directories or target types, reduces noise and improves precision.

Dead Code Discovery

Unused or "dead" code increases build time and maintenance overhead. Identifying such code in a Bazel workspace involves detecting targets not referenced by any other target, except for root entry points (e.g., application binaries and tests).

Targets with zero inbound dependencies are candidates for dead code, excluding those explicitly invoked as build entry points. Using Bazel queries, one can locate these targets by defining root sets and filtering. For example:

```
bazel query "kind('.*_binary|.*_test', //...)" > roots.txt
bazel query "buildfiles(//...)" > all_targets.txt
bazel query "all_targets except deps(set(roots.txt))" >
    dead_targets.txt
```

The above sequence extracts the root build targets, enumerates all targets, and finds those not reachable from any root, indicating dead code. Further refinement considers generated targets and tool outputs to minimize false positives.

Build Optimization Through Query-Driven Insights

Insights from dependency graph querying enable improvements in build performance and organization. Some practical optimizations include:

- Reducing large transitive dependency closures: Querying transitive dependencies for critical targets reveals opaque dependencies that extend build durations. Refactoring those dependencies into finer-grained targets or separating public and private APIs can confine rebuild scope.

- Identifying unnecessary test execution: Queries pinpoint tests indirectly depending on unrelated code changes. Redesigning dependency boundaries reduces test execution for isolated changes.

- Detecting cyclic dependencies: While Bazel prohibits cycles in the build graph, query inconsistencies and suspicious bidirectional dependencies hint at problematic configurations. Queries aid in detecting such patterns before they escalate.

- Analyzing shared library usage: For large codebases, understanding which targets share libraries informs caching and cache invalidation strategies.

One advanced query technique utilizes regular expressions and predicates to isolate specific dependency patterns. For example, to identify all Java libraries in a package that depend on a common utility library:

```
bazel query 'kind("java_library", deps(//common:util)) intersect
    //myproject/...'
```

Such targeted queries optimize the dependency graph's maintenance and evolve alongside the codebase.

Best Practices in Workflow Integration

Incorporating Bazel queries into automated build and continuous integration pipelines extends real-time feedback on code health. For instance, as a pre-submit check, queries can flag unexpectedly large dependency expansions or detect newly introduced dead code.

Automation can harness the query output in machine-readable formats, such as `--output=proto` or `--output=jsonproto`, for integration with custom analysis tools and dashboards. Visualizing the incremental changes in the dependency graph between commits aids informed decision-making.

Summary of Key Query Commands

`deps(<target>)`	Recursively shows all dependencies of the specified target.
`rdeps(<scope>, <target>)`	Finds all targets in `<scope>` depending on `<target>`.
`kind(<kind>, <scope>)`	Filters targets by the rule kind within a scope.
`attr(<attribute>=<value>, <scope>)`	Filters targets by attribute value.
`buildfiles(<scope>)`	Lists all targets defined in build files in scope.
`labels(<pattern>, <scope>)`	Finds targets matching label patterns.
`allpaths(<start>, <end>)`	Displays all paths between two targets for dependency tracing.

These commands, combined with Boolean and set operations supported by Bazel queries, enable constructing precise inquiries suited to diverse analysis needs.

Bazel's built-in query tools form a powerful arsenal for deep dependency graph analysis. Mastery of these tools facilitates impact analysis, dead code discovery, and build optimization in complex codebases, ultimately yielding faster, more reliable, and maintainable builds.

4.2. Managing Transitive and Diamond Dependencies

Transitive dependencies arise when a project depends on a package that itself depends on other packages, creating a hierarchical chain of dependencies. While this mechanism promotes modularity and code reuse, it introduces complexity that can lead to common challenges such as diamond dependencies, version conflicts, and dependency cycles. Managing these effectively is critical for maintaining a stable and predictable software build.

A *diamond dependency* occurs when two or more packages depend on a common sub-package, but potentially on different versions or configurations of that sub-package, forming a dependency graph resembling a diamond shape. Consider a project $\mathcal{P}$ depending on packages $\mathcal{A}$ and $\mathcal{B}$, where both $\mathcal{A}$ and $\mathcal{B}$ depend on package $\mathcal{C}$. If $\mathcal{A}$ requires version 1.0 of $\mathcal{C}$ while $\mathcal{B}$ requires version 2.0, the build system confronts a conflict. Without careful management, this discrepancy can cause build failures, runtime incompatibilities, or subtle bugs.

Version conflicts extend beyond diamond structures and may appear anywhere in the dependency graph. They reflect cases where multiple dependent packages demand incompatible versions of a shared dependency. Such conflicts fall into two principal categories:

- *Direct conflicts*, where different dependency paths impose mutually exclusive version requirements on the same package.

- *Indirect conflicts*, where transitive dependencies introduce incompatible versions indirectly.

Both forms complicate dependency resolution and, if unresolved, jeopardize binary compatibility or lead to redundant package duplication.

Dependency cycles constitute another class of critical problems. Cycles occur when package dependencies form a closed loop, e.g., $\mathcal{X} \rightarrow \mathcal{Y} \rightarrow \mathcal{Z} \rightarrow \mathcal{X}$. Cyclic dependencies threaten build determinism and may prevent certain build actions, including incremental compilation or static linking, from completing correctly. In well-structured software ecosystems, such cycles are usually avoided or carefully broken through design patterns or tooling support.

Mitigation strategies for these challenges combine design discipline, tooling, and versioning policies. The first essential strategy is to enforce *dependency version alignment*. This involves consolidating versions of shared dependencies across the dependency graph to a single compatible version. Dependency management tools often provide mechanisms such as `dependency overrides`, `resolution strategies`, or `dependency constraints` to control versions centrally. For example, in Maven, `dependencyManagement` ensures consistent transitive versions; in npm, `npm dedupe` helps minimize version duplication.

Another effective approach is *preferential flattening* of dependency graphs, where the build system attempts to reduce deep dependency chains by promoting common dependencies to the top level. Flattening can eliminate redundant versions by unifying them early in the resolution process, thus simplifying the dependency namespace and reducing conflicts. However, flattening requires careful consideration to avoid breaking backward compatibility or package encapsulation integrity.

Dependency cycles must be detected early. Static analysis tools integrated into build pipelines can identify cycles and flag them to developers for correction. Once detected, cycle resolution typically involves refactoring to decouple components. Common patterns include introducing abstractions or interfaces to invert dependencies or splitting large packages into smaller, orthogonal libraries. This process enhances modularity and breaks harmful circular references.

In contexts where strict alignment or flattening is infeasible due to incompatible versions, *isolation techniques* can alleviate issues. For instance, Java's `ClassLoader` or .NET's `Assembly Load Context` allow loading multiple versions of the same library side-by-side in isolated runtime environments. Containerized or microservices architectures also enable version isolation at the deployment level, avoiding conflicts in runtime but increasing operational complexity.

Careful semantic versioning (SemVer) plays a pivotal role in reducing conflicts proactively. SemVer prescribes how versions are incremented based on backward compatibility, enabling tools to infer compatible upgrades automatically and warn about potential breaking changes. Libraries that faithfully follow SemVer reduce collision frequency, as dependency resolvers can select compatible upgrades without manual intervention. Additionally, *strict enforcement of version ranges* in dependency descriptors further constrains transitive dependencies to safe versions.

A useful illustrative example in the npm ecosystem demonstrates resolving diamond dependency conflicts:

```
{
  "dependencies": {
    "A": "^1.0.0",
    "B": "^1.0.0"
  }
}
```

Assuming:

- Package A@1.0.0 depends on C@1.2.0.

- Package B@1.0.0 depends on C@2.0.0.

A version conflict arises for C. The developer can resolve this by explicitly adding C at the top level with a compatible version, such as:

```
{
  "dependencies": {
    "A": "^1.0.0",
    "B": "^1.0.0",
    "C": "2.0.0"
  }
}
```

This instructs the package manager to override transitive versions and unify the dependency, assuming compatibility.

Monitoring and auditing dependency graphs is essential. Tools such as Maven Enforcer Plugin, npm ls, yarn-deduplicate,

`Bundler Audit`, or `pipdeptree` provide insights into the resolved dependency tree, highlighting conflicts, cycles, and redundancies. Integrating these into continuous integration pipelines ensures early detection and mitigation of dependency issues before they affect production releases.

Managing transitive and diamond dependencies requires a multifaceted approach: enforcing version alignment, detecting and resolving cycles, employing isolation where necessary, and leveraging rigorous semantic versioning. Robust dependency management tools and practices transform complex dependency graphs into manageable, predictable systems, maintaining build stability and facilitating scalable software evolution.

4.3. Handling External Dependencies at Scale

Managing external dependencies at scale poses a distinct set of challenges that extend beyond the capabilities of basic package management techniques. In expansive enterprise environments or large-scale projects, the multiplicity and diversity of external artifacts-ranging from third-party libraries to internal shared repositories-require robust strategies for importing, pinning, updating, and reproducing these dependencies with precision, security, and consistency.

At its core, scalable dependency management must balance flexibility with control. Ad hoc or uncontrolled dependency imports jeopardize reproducibility, increase the risk of supply chain attacks, and complicate auditability. Thus, a disciplined approach to specifying, resolving, and maintaining external artifacts is critical.

Pinning Dependencies for Reproducibility

Pinning refers to the act of fixing a dependency to a specific version, commit hash, or artifact checksum, thereby ensuring that builds and deployments are deterministic. In large-scale environments,

relying solely on semantic version ranges or latest tags is insuffi-
cient, as these may inadvertently introduce breaking changes or
vulnerabilities.

Effective pinning strategies include:

- **Immutable Version References**: Utilize exact version
  numbers, commit hashes, or content-addressable identifiers
  (e.g., SHA-256 digests) rather than floating tags such as
  latest. This guarantees that every build references a known
  artifact state.

- **Lockfiles**: Centralized lockfiles track the resolved versions
  of all transitive dependencies. These files enable repeatable
  installs and serve as a single source of truth for dependency
  resolution.

- **Artifact Digest Verification**: Beyond version pinning,
  cryptographic hash verification ensures integrity against
  tampering or corruption. Artifact registries and package
  managers increasingly support digest-based resolution as a
  security best practice.

Automated and Policy-Driven Update Mechanisms

While pinning maintains stability, systems must accommodate updates to remedy security vulnerabilities, fix bugs, or incorporate
new features. For enterprise-scale dependency management, updates require coordination, validation, and auditing to prevent disruption.

Scalable approaches for managing updates include:

- **Automated Dependency Scanning and Notification**:
  Employ tools that continuously monitor dependency versions and notify relevant teams of available updates, security
  patches, or license changes.

- **Staged Rollouts and Canary Releases**: Integrate update testing in isolated or limited environments before broader propagation, allowing verification of compatibility and performance.

- **Policy-Driven Update Pipelines**: Define rules governing when and how dependencies may be updated, incorporating criteria such as severity of vulnerabilities, backward compatibility guarantees, or stakeholder approvals.

- **Version Range Constraints with Overrides**: For transitive dependencies, use conservative version constraints coupled with explicit overrides where necessary, preventing inadvertent resolution to incompatible or unsafe versions.

Centralized Dependency Management Systems

At enterprise scale, managing hundreds or thousands of dependencies facilitated across multiple projects demands centralized infrastructure. Such systems consolidate metadata, enforce policies, and provide unified visibility.

Key features of centralized management systems include:

- **Private Artifact Repositories and Proxy Caches**: Hosting internal mirrors or proxies for external repositories reduces external exposure and improves availability while enabling control over artifacts.

- **Dependency Governance Dashboards**: Comprehensive tracking of which projects depend on which artifacts, including their versions, update status, and risk assessments.

- **Access Controls and Auditing**: Role-based access controls ensure only authorized personnel can modify dependency configurations or approve updates; audit logs support compliance and forensic analysis.

Reproducible Builds with Immutable Environments

Large-scale dependency management must be integrated with reproducible build environments to guarantee that artifacts can be reconstructed reliably, regardless of temporal or infrastructural changes.

Best practices include:

- **Immutable Build Containers**: Employ containerized or sandboxed build environments that encapsulate pinned dependencies and build tools, preventing drift caused by host system changes.

- **Declarative Dependency Specifications**: Utilize manifests (e.g., `package.json`, `requirements.txt`, or custom registry schemas) that explicitly enumerate all dependencies and their versions.

- **Dependency Graph Locking**: Tools that generate and consume the entire dependency graph representation, including transitive dependencies, facilitate end-to-end reproducibility.

Scaling Dependency Resolution with Parallelism and Caching

Handling dependencies across numerous projects concurrently increases demands on network bandwidth, storage, and resolution latency. Optimizations to accelerate dependency resolution and artifact retrieval are essential.

Techniques include:

- **Parallel Fetching and Resolution**: Modern package managers support parallel downloads and concurrent resolution of independent dependency subgraphs, reducing total resolution time.

- **Layered Caching Architectures**: Local caches on developer machines combined with shared network caches minimize redundant fetching from external sources.

- **Incremental Resolution**: Cache metadata and partial resolution states to avoid recomputing entire graphs when only minor dependency changes occur.

Security and Compliance Considerations

At scale, external dependencies introduce significant attack surfaces. Security must be embedded in every phase of dependency management:

- **Artifact Signing and Verification**: Encouraging or enforcing signed packages and cryptographic verification prevents supply-chain compromises.

- **Vulnerability Scanning**: Continuous scanning of dependencies for known vulnerabilities, licensing issues, and outdated components ensures proactive risk mitigation.

- **Dependency Blacklisting and Approval Lists**: Central policies may disallow use of certain repositories, packages, or versions based on risk assessments or compliance constraints.

Example: Declarative Pinning via a Lockfile

Consider a JSON-formatted lockfile encapsulating pinned dependencies, including checksums:

```
{
  "dependencies": {
    "libraryA": {
      "version": "2.4.3",
      "resolved": "https://repo.example.com/libraryA-2.4.3.tgz",
```

```
    "integrity": "sha256-3a5f675a8f8b89e20e0917f0cd7b4a0a2c0b2
    ..."
  },
  "libraryB": {
    "version": "1.8.0",
    "resolved": "https://repo.example.com/libraryB-1.8.0.tgz",
    "integrity": "sha256-98f96372aa0cd3d7b0f24bb5c9a1c1f7e2d4
    ..."
  }
 }
}
```

The exact `resolved` URLs and `integrity` hashes ensure that any consumer of this lockfile retrieves precisely the intended artifact versions, fostering reproducibility and security.

Summary of Best Practices

- Always enforce exact pins with checksums or immutable references.

- Harness lockfiles or centralized registries as authoritative sources.

- Incorporate continuous monitoring and controlled update workflows.

- Employ private proxies and access control to protect internal operations.

- Integrate reproducible build environments to guarantee artifact fidelity.

- Optimize resolution scalability through caching and parallelism.

- Prioritize security by verifying signatures, scanning for vulnerabilities, and enforcing policy compliance.

Taken together, these practices form a comprehensive methodology for handling external dependencies in large-scale environments, facilitating reliable builds, secure supply chains, and maintainable ecosystems.

4.4. Version Pinning and Lockfiles

Software projects frequently depend on external libraries and modules, creating complex dependency graphs that evolve as individual packages update independently. To maintain stability, it is crucial to ensure that the precise versions of dependencies remain consistent across development environments, testing setups, continuous integration (CI) pipelines, and production deployments. Version pinning and lockfiles are essential mechanisms employed to guarantee reproducible builds and predictable software behavior.

Version pinning refers to the explicit specification of exact versions for each dependency, rather than allowing flexible version ranges. This practice prevents unintended upgrades, which may introduce incompatibilities or regressions. Pinning can be done in different formats, for instance, in `pip` requirements files using the "equal to" operator:

```
requests==2.28.1
numpy==1.23.0
```

Here, `requests==2.28.1` fixes the version of the `requests` library precisely. Pinning ensures that every environment installs the same upstream release of each package, eliminating variability arising from semver-compatible or rolling updates.

However, specifying fixed versions for direct dependencies alone does not guarantee complete reproducibility. Transitive dependencies-those dependencies required by direct dependencies-may still vary if their versions are loosely specified. This necessitates the use of lockfiles, which capture the entire resolved dependency graph, including all transitive packages with explicit versions and checksums where possible. Lockfiles act as snapshots of the full dependency closure at a given point in time.

Common tools generate and persist lockfiles automatically as part of the package management workflow. For example, `pipenv` produces a `Pipfile.lock` with a canonical listing of resolved packages, while npm uses `package-lock.json`, yarn employs `yarn.lock`, and `Cargo` for Rust creates `Cargo.lock`. These lockfiles serve as authoritative references for package installers, instructing them to replicate installations exactly.

The lockfile format typically catalogs each resolved package's name, locked version, source URL or registry, and cryptographic hash of the downloaded artifact (e.g., SHA256). The inclusion of hashes adds another layer of assurance, detecting tampering or corruption in packages fetched remotely:

```
{
  "name": "requests",
  "version": "2.28.1",
  "hashes": ["sha256:8ce0363c..."],
  "dependencies": {
    "certifi": "2022.12.7",
    "charset-normalizer": "3.0.1"
  }
}
```

Strictly honoring the lockfile during installation guarantees that all environments are identical in terms of dependency trees and artifacts. This uniformity eliminates "works on my machine" issues and reduces integration problems that arise from divergent dependency versions.

In collaborative settings with multiple developers working simultaneously, a lockfile facilitates synchronization of dependency state. When a dependency is updated, the updated lockfile is committed to version control alongside application code. Subsequent environment setup commands consult the lockfile to install the exact dependencies without introducing silent drift.

In the context of CI pipelines, enforcing lockfile-based installs enables repeatable and deterministic builds. CI agents execute automated tests against stable, known-good dependency sets, ensuring that any test failures or regressions are attributable only to application changes, not unseen package updates. The lockfile thus becomes a contract for dependency integrity across distributed systems.

Despite these advantages, version pinning and lockfiles must be maintained conscientiously. Stale lockfiles can lead to outdated or vulnerable dependencies persisting in projects. Periodic lockfile regeneration and security audits are recommended to incorporate updates and patches while preserving compatibility.

Figure illustrates the typical version pinning and lockfile-enabled development workflow, highlighting synchronization points and dependency resolution:

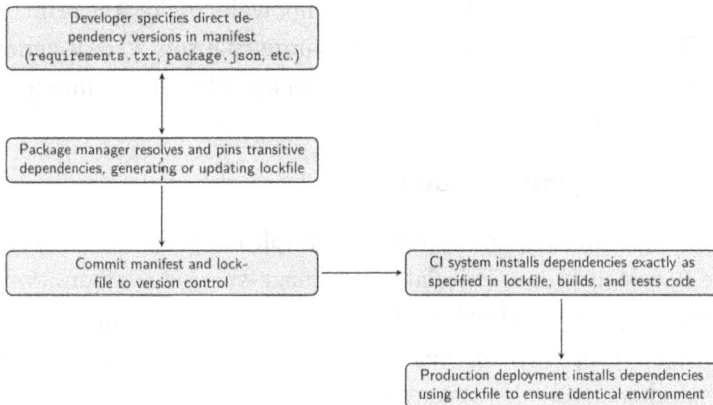

Developer specifies direct dependency versions in manifest (`requirements.txt`, `package.json`, etc.)

↓

Package manager resolves and pins transitive dependencies, generating or updating lockfile

↓

Commit manifest and lockfile to version control → CI system installs dependencies exactly as specified in lockfile, builds, and tests code

↓

Production deployment installs dependencies using lockfile to ensure identical environment

Ultimately, version pinning combined with lockfile inclusion ensures that every phase of a software lifecycle operates on a stable, verified dependency baseline, thus reducing risk and improving maintainability. These practices are indispensable for scaling teams, complex projects, and continuous deployment workflows where predictability and consistency are paramount.

4.5. Polyglot and Cross-language Builds

Managing polyglot codebases introduces both opportunities and complexities in modern software development, and Bazel's build system offers robust mechanisms to address these challenges. Polyglot projects, comprising components written in multiple programming languages, require careful handling of build configurations, rule selection, and interoperability layers to ensure efficient and reliable build outputs.

At its core, Bazel enforces a strict dependency graph, enabling deterministic and reproducible builds across diverse languages. Each language ecosystem integrates through a specific set of Bazel rules, which encapsulate language-specific build logic, compiler invocations, linking, and packaging. For polyglot builds, the primary challenge is harmonizing these disparate rule sets so that generated artifacts can properly interface, share data, and maintain coherent build semantics.

Configuring Polyglot Builds

A fundamental step in supporting multiple languages within a single Bazel workspace is isolating language-specific configurations. This is typically realized by defining language toolchains and selecting appropriate rulesets. Toolchains in Bazel abstract compilers, linkers, and other essential tooling. Setting them up correctly ensures that each language's requirements are met while allowing Bazel to reason about cross-language dependencies effectively.

Consider a codebase containing C++, Java, and Python components. The workspace might include the following key configurations:

- `@bazel_tools//tools/cpp:toolchain_config` for native C++ compiler selection.

- `@rules_java//java:defs.bzl` for Java rule implementations and toolchains.

- `@rules_python//python:defs.bzl` for Python packaging and runtime environment.

The `WORKSPACE` file integrates these repositories, ensuring correct versions and dependencies are synchronized. In some cases, custom toolchain definitions may be necessary to accommodate proprietary or specialized build tools. This modular design supports incremental extension as new languages or tools are introduced into the codebase.

Rule Selection and Composition

The essence of polyglot building lies in selecting appropriate Bazel rules for each language target and composing their outputs. Each language provides a native abstraction of libraries, binaries, and tests, but integration points must be explicitly established. The following outlines typical approaches for combining language outputs:

- **Static and Shared Libraries**: C++ libraries often serve as native dependencies for other languages via Foreign Function Interfaces (FFI). They are declared using `cc_library` and produce static (`.a`) or shared (`.so`/`.dll`) libraries.

- **Java JARs and Targets**: The `java_library` and `java_binary` rules generate JAR artifacts and executable JVM bytecode. Java can consume JNI bindings to native C++ libraries for performance-critical operations.

- **Python Packages**: The `py_library` and `py_binary` rules encapsulate Python sources and dependencies. Python extensions written in C/C++ are typically wrapped with Bazel `cc_library` targets and interfaced through Python's native modules or extension APIs.

To illustrate, consider a Python application requiring a C++ extension and a Java-based backend service:

```
cc_library(
    name = "fastmath",
    srcs = ["fastmath.cc"],
    hdrs = ["fastmath.h"],
    visibility = ["//visibility:public"],
)

py_library(
    name = "pyfastmath",
    srcs = ["pyfastmath.py"],
    deps = [":fastmath"],
)

java_binary(
    name = "backend_service",
    srcs = glob(["backend/**/*.java"]),
    deps = ["//libs/common", "//third_party:some_java_dep"],
)
```

Here, the Python library depends on the C++ extension, potentially exported via a Python C extension interface. Bazel guarantees that fastmath is built prior to pyfastmath, ensuring proper linkage and runtime consistency.

Interoperability Nuances

Cross-language interoperability is constrained by differences in compilation, runtime semantics, and data representation. Bazel facilitates integration but does not abstract away language-specific complexities. Careful engineering is required to address these areas:

- **ABI Compatibility**: Ensuring Application Binary Interface (ABI) consistency between C++ libraries and consumers is vital. Compiler flags, calling conventions, and platform-specific differences must be managed within Bazel toolchain configurations to prevent subtle errors.

- **Data Serialization Formats**: When languages communicate through serialized data (e.g., Protocol Buffers, Apache

Thrift), Bazel rules for code generation produce source artifacts in multiple languages from a single schema definition. This ensures versioning consistency and reduces manual synchronization.

- **Build Artifact Linking**: Linking native and managed code requires explicit wrappers or bridging layers, e.g., JNI for Java and C++, ctypes or cffi for Python and C/C++. Bazel supports these by allowing custom build steps or genrules that generate glue code as part of the build graph.

Cross-language Testing and Validation

Testing polyglot builds is complicated by runtime differences and integration points where languages interact. Bazel's test rules (cc_test, java_test, py_test) enable language-specific testing, but end-to-end cross-language tests may require orchestrated environments or harnesses.

A common practice involves:

- Isolating unit tests per language to focus on language-local correctness.

- Creating integration tests as build targets that invoke binaries or scripts exercising the interoperability layers.

- Embedding runtime environment setup in sh_test or custom test rules to simulate multi-language invocation and data flow.

Bazel's sandboxing and parallel execution capabilities ensure these tests are hermetic, reproducible, and isolate side effects, critical for large-scale polyglot systems.

Challenges and Best Practices

Polyglot builds with Bazel are powerful yet present specific challenges:

- **Rule Ecosystem Maturity**: Not all languages have equally mature Bazel rules or toolchain integrations. This can necessitate custom rule development or extensions.

- **Performance Overhead**: Complex inter-language dependencies may lengthen build times due to conservative invalidation of dependent targets. Fine-grained dependency declarations and caching strategies mitigate this risk.

- **Debugging Complexity**: Diagnosing build or runtime errors across language boundaries demands detailed awareness of each language's tooling, as well as the Bazel build graph.

Adhering to modular target structures, maintaining strict visibility scopes, and leveraging code generation tools enhance maintainability. Continuous integration pipelines integrating Bazel's build and test phases further ensure polyglot system robustness.

Bazel's design fundamentally supports polyglot codebases through its extensible rule system, strict dependency graph, and configurable toolchains. The ability to compose language-specific rules and enforce hermetic builds empowers development teams to build, test, and deploy complex, multi-language applications with high confidence. Mastery of configuration nuances, interoperability layers, and testing strategies is essential to fully exploit Bazel's capabilities in polyglot environments.

4.6. Custom Repository Types and Mirrors

The integration of custom repository types within modern build and artifact management systems addresses imperative requirements of enterprise-scale development environments, particularly concerning compliance, availability, and security. Custom repositories extend beyond traditional public or centralized repositories by enabling tailored functionality suited to local regulations, network optimization, and secure supply chain management. This section elaborates on the architecture, implementation strategies, and operational considerations for custom repository types and local mirrors that play pivotal roles in sustaining enterprise compliance and enhancing build reproducibility.

Rationale for Custom Repository Types

Enterprises often encounter constraints that standard public repositories cannot satisfy, including data sovereignty laws, proprietary code restrictions, or network segmentation policies. Custom repository types serve as controlled endpoints for artifact storage and distribution, allowing firms to encapsulate tailored policies like authentication schemas, metadata enrichment, and auditing. By implementing such repositories, organizations achieve a trustworthy source of components while preventing unauthorized access or leakage of sensitive materials.

Moreover, the traditional reliance on globally distributed public repositories introduces variability due to external infrastructure performance or availability fluctuations, resulting in diminished build determinism. Custom mirrors—local replicas of external repositories—mitigate this risk by caching artifacts proximate to consumption points, thereby decreasing latency and shielding builds from external service interruptions.

Design Considerations and Architectural Components

A robust custom repository system necessitates a modular design capable of interfacing with various artifact storage backends (e.g., object stores, file systems, or database blobs) and supporting metadata management to track provenance and versioning at granular levels. The repository interface should expose standard protocols such as HTTP(S) with RESTful API endpoints, enabling both retrieval and publication of artifacts under stringent access controls.

Key architectural components include:

115

- **Storage Backend:** Persistent and highly available media, potentially distributed, to host artifacts while preserving integrity and immutability policies.

- **Metadata Service:** Maintains detailed records of artifact versions, dependencies, checksums, and compliance attestations, facilitating traceability and auditability.

- **Access Control Layer:** Enforces authentication and authorization rules tailored to enterprise security policies, often integrating with identity providers (e.g., LDAP, OAuth2).

- **Mirror Synchronization Module:** For local mirrors, this component manages replication policies, including scheduling, conflict resolution, and delta updates to minimize bandwidth consumption.

- **Logging and Monitoring System:** Captures comprehensive audit trails and operational metrics crucial for compliance verification and anomaly detection.

Implementation Strategies

Custom repository implementations typically adopt one of the following approaches:

1. Extension of Existing Repository Managers

Popular artifact repository managers such as Nexus Repository, Artifactory, and Apache Archiva support plugin architectures or configuration options to create custom repository types. These platforms already provide foundational features including artifact indexing, security frameworks, and developer tooling integrations. Extending them reduces implementation overhead while benefiting from mature, supported ecosystems.

For example, creating a custom proxy repository in Nexus that enforces an additional authentication mechanism might involve implementing a plugin that intercepts and validates each request before forwarding. Similarly, for local mirrors, scheduled replication tasks can be configured to mirror specific repository segments with filtering rules to comply with data governance policies.

2. Custom Standalone Repository Services

When enterprise requirements demand specialized protocols or advanced compliance mechanisms beyond what existing solutions offer, developing bespoke repository servers becomes pertinent. Such implementations utilize web frameworks, secure storage APIs, and cryptographic libraries to enforce artifact signing and verification natively. These servers may implement fine-grained policy engines that incorporate organizational rules governing artifact acceptance or promotion stages.

The following pseudocode illustrates a simplified artifact upload handler enforcing a policy check before storing the artifact:

```
def handle_upload(request):
    artifact = request.get_file('artifact')
    metadata = extract_metadata(artifact)

    if not policy_compliant(metadata):
        return Response(status=403, body='Artifact does not meet
    compliance policies.')

    store_artifact(artifact, metadata)
    log_upload_event(request.user, metadata)
    return Response(status=201, body='Artifact uploaded
    successfully.')
```

3. Proxy-Based Local Mirrors

Local mirrors serve as intermediaries that transparently cache artifacts fetched from remote repositories. They may operate in a pull-based manner—retrieving artifacts on demand—or use push-based synchronization via scheduled batch updates. To optimize storage and bandwidth, mirrors often implement deduplication and incremental synchronization algorithms.

Robust mirrors ensure cryptographic validation of upstream artifacts, verifying checksums and signatures before caching to prevent supply chain attacks. Additionally, mirrors can quarantine suspicious artifacts awaiting manual inspection to enhance security further.

Security and Compliance Enhancements

Implementing custom repositories and mirrors must factor in strict security measures to safeguard the artifact supply chain. Essential mechanisms include:

- **Artifact Signing and Verification:** Enforce the use of digital signatures on artifacts using standards such as PGP or X.509 certificates. Verification at consumption or mirror points ensures artifact authenticity and integrity.

- **Immutable Artifact Promotion Pipelines:** Enforce repository immutability rules whereby once artifacts are published, they cannot be altered or deleted, supporting reproducibility and forensic capabilities.

- **Access Auditing and Provenance Tracking:** Maintain detailed logs linking users, actions, and artifacts to prove compliance in audit scenarios and detect anomalous activities.

- **Policy-Based Access and Distribution Controls:** Deploy fine-grained access control lists (ACLs) and conditional release mechanisms aligned with regulatory requirements such as ITAR, GDPR, or HIPAA.

Build Reproducibility via Controlled Repository Environments

Custom repositories decisively improve build reproducibility by offering deterministic artifact resolution. They enable:

- **Fixed Artifact Snapshots:** Pinning builds to specific repository snapshots eliminates variability introduced by mutable artifact versions or external repository changes.

- **Hermetic Builds:** By relying exclusively on local mirrors or private artifact servers, builds avoid transient network dependencies, thereby increasing stability and build speed.

- **Consistent Dependency Resolution:** Custom metadata services may integrate dependency locking mechanisms ensuring uniform dependency graphs across different environments.

Integrating such controlled repository systems with build tools and continuous integration pipelines amplifies the overall supply chain security posture and provides reliable traceability from source code to deployed binaries.

Case Example: Enterprise Mirror Synchronization Workflow

Consider an enterprise engineering organization that implements daily synchronization from public Maven Central to a private Nexus Repository mirror, constrained by corporate firewall policies and stringent compliance controls. The synchronization process follows these steps:

```
1. Trigger scheduled synchronization job overnight.
2. Validate repository configurations and access tokens.
3. For each designated public repository path:
   a. Download new or updated artifact metadata.
   b. Verify cryptographic signatures and checksums.
   c. Fetch the artifact payload if verification succeeds.
   d. Reject and quarantine any non-compliant artifacts.
4. Update internal metadata catalogs to reflect latest synchronized artifacts
   .
5. Audit log generation and alert on discrepancies.
6. Notify stakeholders upon synchronization completion.
```

This workflow ensures that all developers within the organization operate against a consistent, secure, and compliant artifact repository, effectively mitigating risks endemic to direct external dependency resolution.

Through the strategic deployment of custom repository types and mirrors, enterprises substantially enhance their control over the software supply chain, ensuring that the artifacts powering their builds are trustworthy, accessible, and compliant. These capabilities are indispensable for maintaining robust supply chain security and enabling reproducible software engineering practices at scale.

Chapter 5

Scalability and Performance Optimization

When every second shaved from a build translates to developer happiness and product velocity, mastering Bazel's scaling and speed is not optional—it's transformational. This chapter reveals the best-kept secrets behind lightning-fast builds at any scale, from action graph optimization to distributed remote execution. Learn how the world's largest engineering organizations turn Bazel into a competitive advantage for both productivity and maintainability.

5.1. Optimizing the Action Graph

The action graph in Bazel encapsulates the comprehensive set of build actions and their dependencies that must be executed to produce the desired output artifacts. Optimizing this graph requires minimizing redundancy among actions and pruning unnecessary dependencies, thereby reducing build times and improving parallel execution efficiency. Central to this effort is a detailed analysis of how actions are generated and interconnected, ensuring that the graph structure supports maximal concurrency without redundant computations or dependency bloat.

A primary source of redundancy in the action graph arises when multiple targets depend on overlapping, yet distinct sets of inputs, resulting in duplicated actions or excessive intermediate artifacts. In such scenarios, Bazel's design encourages structuring BUILD files and rules to exploit shared outputs and encapsulate reusable components effectively. For instance, consolidating common pre-processing or compilation steps into a single rule and exporting its outputs reduces redundant processing. This consolidation is reflected in the action graph as shared nodes and edges, enabling Bazel's scheduler to invoke actions once and serve all dependents.

Dependency bloat often manifests through overly broad or transitive dependencies in target specifications. Explicitly declared dependencies that are not tightly scoped can pull unnecessary targets into the build, expanding the action graph size disproportionately. To counteract this, employing attribute-level visibility control and dependency pruning techniques is recommended. Strategically using Bazel's `deps` and `data` attributes to distinguish between compile-time and runtime dependencies, along with leveraging `select()` expressions for config-specific dependencies, helps constrain the action graph. This reduction is critical when working with large monolithic repositories where unchecked transitive closure can balloon the graph exponentially.

Analyzing the action graph efficiently requires profiling and visualization tools capable of exposing bottlenecks and redundant action patterns. Bazel provides command-line options such as `bazel build --experimental_graphviz_dump`, which outputs the action graph in Graphviz format. This format can be transformed into node-link diagrams highlighting action dependencies and concurrency opportunities. By examining the resulting graph, engineers can identify clusters of actions that share inputs or outputs redundantly and pinpoint critical paths that dominate build latency.

```
bazel build //my:target --experimental_graphviz_dump=graph.dot
dot -Tpng graph.dot -o graph.png
```

Inspecting the graph visualization facilitates targeted optimizations such as refactoring rule implementations to split monolithic actions into smaller, more granular tasks. Granularity allows Bazel's scheduler to better parallelize execution, increasing utilization across available CPU cores. Furthermore, grouping logically related source inputs and actions encourages cache hits by preventing minor input changes from triggering unnecessary rebuilds of unrelated components.

Action graph optimization can also be achieved by minimizing the number of declared inputs per action without affecting correctness. Since Bazel uses action inputs to determine cache validity and incremental build correctness, extraneous inputs force unnecessary invalidations. For example, tools that generate outputs during execution may declare more inputs than strictly needed, thereby causing cascading rebuilds. Careful auditing of input declarations in the rule's implementation and build scripts can remove such superfluous dependencies.

An advanced technique involves custom Skylark rules that encapsulate complex build logic while exposing minimal inputs and precise outputs. These user-defined rules enable fine-tuned control over the action graph. For example, combining multiple lightweight tools or scripts into a single action with carefully managed inputs can decrease the total number of actions. However, this process involves balancing action granularity with increased tool complexity, as overly broad actions reduce incremental build benefits.

High parallelism in the action graph is realized through maximizing the number of actions that can run concurrently without interdependencies. This is facilitated by ensuring acyclic and finely segmented dependency edges. Cyclic dependencies introduce build failures and dependency cycles, while overly coarse dependencies serialize the build unnecessarily. Static analysis of BUILD files for circular dependencies and modularization of targets into smaller, cohesive units supports maintaining a well-formed action graph.

Moreover, Bazel's feature of sandboxing actions enforces hermetic execution by isolating inputs, which permits more aggressive parallelism safely. By guaranteeing reproducibility through sandboxing, the build system can schedule dependent actions freely with no hidden interference risks, thus fully leveraging multicore machines.

Overall strategies for optimizing the Bazel action graph include:

- **Consolidation of common actions:** Refactor build rules to merge duplicate processing steps, reducing redundant executions.

- **Pruning dependency declarations:** Tighten deps and data to minimize transitive bloat.

- **Analyzing action graphs:** Utilize Graphviz and profiling tools to identify bottlenecks and redundant subgraphs.

- **Fine-grained rule design:** Craft Skylark rules that balance action granularity and caching efficiency.

- **Ensuring acyclic and minimal dependencies:** Prevent build graph cycles and overly broad edges that limit parallelism.

- **Leverage sandboxing:** Employ Bazel's sandbox isolation to improve correctness and concurrency.

Optimizing the action graph effectively unlocks performance gains by enabling Bazel to execute more actions in parallel, reducing total build latency and maximizing resource utilization. This results in faster, more reliable builds, which is particularly critical for large-scale, complex projects. The synergy of disciplined build rule engineering, dependency management, and tooling-assisted graph inspection forms the foundation of a robust action graph optimization methodology.

5.2. Profiling and Bottleneck Identification

Profiling Bazel builds is pivotal for optimizing complex projects where incremental build speed and resource utilization determine overall productivity. The process begins by gathering detailed performance data through Bazel's built-in profiling mechanisms. This data provides insights into the temporal and resource distribution patterns across the entire build pipeline, enabling systematic hotspot detection and informed optimization decisions.

Bazel supports comprehensive profiling via the `--profile` flag, which generates a performance trace file capturing detailed timing information for individual build execution phases, rule actions, dependency resolution, and cache interactions. The typical invocation involves specifying a file path for the profile output:

```
bazel build //target --profile=profile.gz
```

The resulting `profile.gz` file contains a gzip-compressed protobuf trace encoding a wealth of performance data. To interpret this data, Bazel provides auxiliary tools such as `bazel analyze-profile`, which converts the raw trace into human-readable summaries and flame graphs that visualize execution hotspots:

```
bazel analyze-profile profile.gz
```

The output organizes statistics along logical dimensions such as build phases (loading, analysis, execution), individual actions, and target-specific breakdowns. Prioritizing hotspots requires understanding the relative time consumption and frequency of actions, focusing particularly on those with the highest cumulative latency or resource contention.

One critical dimension is the identification of rule actions that incur disproportionate build time, often caused by expensive computations, redundant work, or inefficient tools invoked in rule implementations. Profiling enables the correlation between targets and slow actions, facilitating targeted refactoring or replacement of costly build steps. For instance, if compilation actions dominate the profile, options include optimizing compiler flags, parallelizing compilation units, or leveraging aggressive caching mechanisms.

Beyond action profiling, build metrics also expose bottlenecks in Bazel's internal dependency analysis and graph evaluation processes. Excessive transitive dependency evaluations, complex macros, or redundant attribute computations may inflate loading and analysis phases. Profiling this segment highlights suboptimal Skylark rules or overly dynamic configurations that hinder Bazel's ability to cache and incrementally evaluate build state.

Memory consumption and garbage collection overhead are additional facets revealed during profiling, especially for large-scale builds. Excessive memory usage often correlates with extensive state retention across build invocations, which can be alleviated by optimizing rule implementations to minimize object lifetimes and data duplication. Monitoring JVM flags, heap consumption, and garbage collection pauses is vital for builds incorporating custom Java-based rule implementations or extensive analysis logic.

Systematic elimination of identified bottlenecks proceeds iteratively, often requiring a combination of approaches:

- **Caching Improvements:** Intensifying use of remote or local caching reduces redundant rebuilds. Profiling reveals cache miss rates by inspecting action cache hit ratios, which guide whether to optimize cache keys or caching infrastructure.

- **Parallelism Tuning:** Adjusting `--jobs` and resource constraints impacts thread and action concurrency, balanced against hardware topology and I/O throughput. Profiling identifies underutilized parallelism opportunities or saturation points causing contention.

- **Rule Optimization:** Refactoring slow rules to eliminate unnecessary environment variable propagation, reduce script overhead, or modularize monolithic actions prevents long-tail build delays. Profiling correlates optimized rules with reduced action duration.

- **Dependency Graph Simplification:** Simplifying or pruning transitive dependencies improves graph evaluation speed. Profiling localizes heavy subgraphs facilitating targeted dependency pruning or splitting.

- **Incremental Build Strategies:** Ensuring build correctness with minimal re-execution involves isolating stable dependencies and managing output directories efficiently. Profiling incremental builds helps validate reduced rebuild scopes and identify regression.

An advanced technique involves integrating external profiling tools such as Linux `perf`, JVM profilers for Skylark execution, or system call tracers to complement Bazel's own profile. Capturing kernel-level events like I/O waits or context switches can explain latency spikes not visible in Bazel's action timelines. Such comprehensive profiling aids in diagnosing systemic bottlenecks like disk contention or suboptimal toolchain invocation patterns.

Profiling outputs should be continuously monitored and compared across build iterations to verify the impact of incremental optimizations. Automated regression detection via build metadata storage enables early detection of performance degradations, preventing hidden bottlenecks from eroding build efficiency over time.

Profiling with Bazel's native tools reveals detailed performance characteristics essential to identifying bottlenecks at action, rule, and dependency graph levels. Through systematic analysis and targeted remediation-encompassing caching strategies, parallelism adjustments, rule simplifications, and dependency management-build efficiency is measurably improved, enabling scalable and maintainable build infrastructures.

5.3. Remote Build Execution and Caching

Remote build execution (RBE) is a paradigm designed to overcome the limitations of local build resources by distributing build tasks across a cluster of remote machines. This architecture enables substantial acceleration of build times, especially for large-scale software projects with complex dependency graphs and resource-intensive compilation steps. At its core, RBE decouples the build task orchestration from the physical compute location, leveraging networked hardware to achieve parallelism and resource optimization unattainable in isolated developer workstations.

The typical RBE system consists of three primary components: the build client, the remote execution service, and the remote cache. The build client generates action requests corresponding to compilation or other build tasks, then dispatches these to the remote execution service. This service schedules the tasks on remote workers-machines configured to execute isolated build actions with guaranteed hermeticity. Upon task completion, results including generated artifacts and metadata are returned to the client. Crucially, the remote cache stores both inputs and outputs of build actions, enabling reuse of previous work either from local or remote sources, thereby avoiding redundant computation.

Architecturally, the RBE infrastructure requires a content-addressable storage (CAS) system, immutable execution environments, and an effective queue and scheduling mechanism. The CAS ensures that artifacts and inputs are addressable by their cryptographic hash, facilitating deduplication and consistency checks. Execution environments are typically containerized or sandboxed to provide hermeticity and reproducibility, preventing side effects and environmental discrepancies from corrupting builds. The scheduler coordinates assigning jobs across available workers, balancing load, prioritizing critical build actions, and handling retries for transient failures.

Maximizing throughput in RBE hinges on careful configuration and tuning of both execution resources and caching strategies. From an infrastructure perspective, worker nodes should be provisioned with heterogeneous capabilities matched to the workload's characteristics: CPU-intensive compilation steps benefit from high core counts, while memory-heavy tasks require nodes with larger RAM capacity. Affinity scheduling optimizes worker assignment based on past execution profiles and data locality, reducing latency by prioritizing workers with cached inputs or outputs relevant to the pending actions.

Remote cache tuning involves calibrating cache policies, capacity, and network parameters to ensure high hit rates and minimal contention. Cache hit rate directly correlates with build acceleration since cache hits eliminate the need for remote execution. To enhance hit rates, it is critical to hash all inputs thoroughly, including compiler options, environment variables, and third-party dependencies, to maintain correctness while maximizing cache reuse potential. Additionally, maintaining a warm cache involves prefetching frequently used artifacts or leveraging continuous integration system integration, where downstream builds utilize upstream build outputs as cache sources.

Configuration best practices recommend isolating build environments to avoid multi-tenancy interference, which can lead to un-predictable performance or cache pollution. Shared build environ-ments should enforce strict sandboxing, immutable base images, and network isolation. Immutable base images ensure consistency in dependencies and operating system libraries, which helps elim-inate non-determinism in builds and increases cache validity. In-strumentation and monitoring of cache metrics provide actionable insights into cache usage patterns, allowing adaptive modifications such as resizing cache storage or evicting stale entries.

Integration of RBE into existing build tools involves plugin or na-tive support to interact with remote execution APIs. For example, build systems such as Bazel or Buck provide built-in mechanisms to specify remote execution endpoints, authentication protocols, and caching scope. Enabling remote execution is typically a con-figuration switch augmented by flags to control upload/download concurrency, size limits, and failure handling strategies (e.g., fall-back to local execution on network errors).

To illustrate, a common remote execution workflow within Bazel entails the following command-line parameters:

```
bazel build //my/package:target \
    --remote_executor=grpc://rbe.example.com:8980 \
    --remote_cache=grpc://cache.example.com:8980 \
    --experimental_remote_downloader \
    --spawn_strategy=remote \
    --strategy=Javac=remote
```

Here, the remote executor and cache endpoints are specified along-side enabling remote downloading of build outputs and setting ex-ecution strategies for specific actions like Java compilation. This approach enables seamless offloading of resource-intensive jobs to the remote infrastructure, while retaining local responsiveness for lightweight tasks.

In practice, the tangible benefits of RBE and caching manifest in significantly reduced average build times, increased developer productivity, and consistent build environments across heterogeneous teams. Still, the complexity of remote infrastructure mandates rigorous security controls including encrypted communication channels, authentication, and authorization scopes to ensure that build artifacts and source code remain confidential and tamper-resistant.

Remote build execution combined with robust caching mechanisms forms an indispensable component of modern, scalable build systems. The architecture's efficacy depends on holistic consideration of resource allocation, cache management, and integration fidelity. Properly attuned, these systems can dramatically compress build cycles, enforce reproducibility, and streamline continuous integration pipelines in large distributed software development environments.

5.4. Incremental Build Acceleration

Bazel's efficiency in handling incremental builds within large-scale codebases fundamentally relies on its ability to precisely identify what must be rebuilt when source changes occur. Unlike traditional build systems that often rely on coarse-grained file timestamps or directory scans, Bazel employs a sophisticated dependency graph with fine-grained invalidation to achieve minimal rebuilds. This approach is rooted in Bazel's model of explicitly declared dependencies and hermetic actions, guaranteeing that only those targets whose inputs have changed or whose dependencies were mutated are subject to rebuild.

At the core of Bazel's incremental build logic is its dependency graph, a directed acyclic graph (DAG) where nodes represent build targets, and edges signify dependency relationships. When a source file or resource is altered, Bazel traverses this graph from the modified nodes upward, marking dependent targets as invalidated. However, crucially, Bazel's invalidation occurs at the level of individual artifacts and intermediate outputs rather than at the coarse granularity of entire projects or directories. This fine-grained invalidation dramatically reduces the scope of rebuilds in gigantic codebases.

The mechanism of determining rebuild necessity leverages content-based hashing of inputs, which include source files, compiler flags, environment variables, and toolchain details. Bazel computes hashes for all inputs associated with each action. If the hash remains consistent since the last build, Bazel reuses the previously generated outputs via the local or remote action cache without rerunning the action. This cache hit reduces rebuild time to the minimum, often just requiring the link step for downstream targets, or no build steps at all.

Cache hits themselves are distinguished into two broad categories: local cache hits and remote cache hits. The local cache stores build artifacts on the developer's machine, enabling instantaneous reuse of prior build outputs in the same workspace. Remote caching and remote execution extend these benefits across teams and CI infrastructures, allowing artifact sharing and distributed parallelism which is critical for extremely large enterprise setups. By maximizing cache hit rates, build latency for incremental changes can be reduced from minutes to seconds, dramatically enhancing developer productivity.

Fine-grained invalidation is complemented by Bazel's action graph analysis, which allows it to understand semantic changes at a granular level. For example, a modification in a header file triggers rebuilding only for those translation units directly or transitively dependent on that header, rather than rebuilding entire libraries or executables indiscriminately. This selective invalidation depends on explicit dependency declarations in BUILD files and ensures that Bazel's paradigm of hermeticity and correctness remains intact.

To fully leverage Bazel's incremental build capabilities, several best practices should be observed. First, dependency declara-

tions should be as precise and minimal as possible to prevent unnecessary rebuild ripple effects. Unintentional transitive dependencies or overly broad target patterns cause superfluous invalidations. Second, defining and maintaining hermetic build actions ensures that outputs are safe to cache and reuse; this includes controlling environment variables, using reproducible compilation flags, and avoiding non-deterministic operations during
builds. Third, enabling remote caching and remote execution infrastructure helps scale incremental builds across large teams and
CI pipelines, where sharing cached artifacts substantially improves
throughput.

Moreover, modularization and proper layering of codebases re-
inforce Bazel's incremental strengths. By structuring code into
fine-grained, well-scoped targets, changes are isolated to smaller
subgraphs of the dependency graph, minimizing rebuild impact.
When the build graph is deep but narrow, Bazel benefits maximally
from incremental compilation and caching.

Another important aspect is the management of generated files
and outputs. Bazel treats generated source files as first-class inputs, tracking their content and recomputing only when upstream
generators produce different results. This feature integrates well
with code generation tools and annotation processors, preventing
global rebuilds induced by minor generated source changes.

Profiling tools integrated into Bazel can assist developers in diagnosing unnecessary rebuilds and improving incremental build performance. Commands such as

```
bazel build --profile=profile.gz //...
```

provide insight into cache hit ratios, action execution times, and
the dependency graph, enabling targeted optimizations. Analysis
of these profiles often highlights inadvertent dependencies, environmental nondeterminism, or suboptimal build rules that can be
improved.

Bazel's incremental build acceleration hinges on the following pillars:

- Explicit dependency graph construction enabling precise invalidation.

- Content-addressable caching ensuring reuse of prior outputs by hash comparison.

- Hermetic and reproducible build actions guaranteeing correctness and cache safety.

- Remote caching and execution extending incremental speeds across distributed environments.

- Target modularization and fine-grained dependencies to reduce rebuild scope.

- Profiling and analysis tools to continually enhance incremental build efficiency.

Adhering to these principles and practices empowers Bazel to deliver near-instantaneous incremental builds even within massive, complex codebases, transforming build latency from a development bottleneck into a negligible overhead.

5.5. Fine-grained Resource Control and Sandboxing

In environments characterized by high concurrency and unpredictable workload patterns, managing resource allocation with precision becomes paramount to maintaining system stability and performance. Fine-grained control over CPU, memory, and I/O resources, combined with robust sandboxing configurations, constitutes the primary defense against the adverse effects of resource contention. These mechanisms ensure both fairness in resource distribution and containment of fault domains, effectively isolating errant processes to protect overall system integrity.

CPU Resource Control Strategies

Fine-grained CPU management in high-concurrency systems entails both reservation and limitation policies that precisely allocate processor cycles to competing workloads. Cgroup v2 (control groups) on Linux systems exemplifies this approach by allowing the division of CPU time via the `cpu.max` parameter, which enforces quota and period constraints on task groups. Implementing proportional-share scheduling through Completely Fair Scheduler (CFS) bandwidth control ensures critical tasks receive guaranteed CPU shares while preventing any single process from monopolizing the CPU.

In asymmetrical multithreading or systems with heterogeneous cores, CPU affinity settings combined with cgroups enable the binding of processes to specific CPUs or cores. This targeted resource control reduces cache thrashing and context-switch overhead, enhancing performance under high concurrency. Schedulers can be fine-tuned with static and dynamic priorities to preempt low-importance workloads when higher priority tasks demand resources.

```
# Mount the cgroup v2 filesystem
mount -t cgroup2 none /sys/fs/cgroup

# Create a new cgroup for a workload
mkdir /sys/fs/cgroup/my_app

# Set CPU maximum quota: 50ms out of 100ms period (50% CPU)
echo "50000 100000" > /sys/fs/cgroup/my_app/cpu.max

# Add a process to the cgroup
echo <pid> > /sys/fs/cgroup/my_app/cgroup.procs
```

Memory Allocation and Isolation

Memory management under heavy workload conditions requires strategies that prevent any single process or group from exhausting system memory, which can precipitate thrashing or out-of-memory kills that degrade service availability. Control groups offer memory.max to cap the maximum allowed memory usage per cgroup, including file cache and anonymous memory.

Beyond absolute limits, soft limits and memory prioritization leverage the Out-Of-Memory (OOM) killer's behavior to safeguard more important workloads. Transparent Huge Pages (THP) and memory compaction mechanisms assist by reducing fragmentation and improving allocation efficiency. Memory pressure monitoring combined with proactive swapping or reclamation triggers adaptive resource throttling before critical thresholds are reached.

Memory namespaces and seccomp filters further sandbox applications by preventing unauthorized inter-process memory access, enforcing strict isolation that defends against both accidental and malicious memory violations.

```
# Set maximum memory usage to 1GB
echo 1073741824 > /sys/fs/cgroup/my_app/memory.max

# Enable kernel memory accounting
echo 1 > /sys/fs/cgroup/my_app/memory.usage_in_bytes

# Add a process to the memory cgroup
echo <pid> > /sys/fs/cgroup/my_app/cgroup.procs
```

I/O Resource Management

High-concurrency environments often experience resource contention on storage and network I/O, which can create bottlenecks and unpredictable latency spikes. Control over I/O bandwidth and priorities is achievable through integrated block I/O controllers (blkio) that regulate request scheduling. The io.max parameter in cgroup v2 enables rate limiting per device and operation type (read/write), ensuring equitable bandwidth shares among competing services.

I/O schedulers like Completely Fair Queuing (CFQ) and Budget Fair Queueing (BFQ) further enhance fairness by dynamically assigning I/O priorities and grouping requests. For network-intensive workloads, traffic control utilities such as tc and eBPF-based filtering enforce rate limits and prioritize critical flows.

Sandboxing techniques also isolate I/O channels to prevent noisy neighbors. For instance, ephemeral file systems (tmpfs) reduce dependency on disk I/O for transient processes, while namespace-based separation facilitates per-application filesystem views, reducing contention points and enhancing security.

```
# Limit read bandwidth on /dev/sda to 10MB/s
echo "8:0 rbps=10485760" > /sys/fs/cgroup/my_app/io.max

# Limit write bandwidth on /dev/sda to 5MB/s
echo "8:0 wbps=5242880" >> /sys/fs/cgroup/my_app/io.max

# Add a process to the I/O cgroup
echo <pid> > /sys/fs/cgroup/my_app/cgroup.procs
```

Sandboxing Configurations Enhancing Stability

Sandboxing not only isolates resource usage but also fortifies system reliability by restricting the scope of faults and malicious actions. Namespaces provide isolation of process IDs, mount points, network interfaces, and IPC mechanisms to create virtualized execution contexts. Combining namespaces with capabilities dropped to the minimum required privileges forms a robust principle of least privilege.

Seccomp filters, configured with Berkeley Packet Filter (BPF) programs, restrict the system calls an application may invoke, limiting the attack surface and potential errant system calls that can negatively impact resource usage. Overlay filesystems enable ephemeral or read-only mounts that prevent processes from altering critical system files or exhausting storage.

Systemd's integration with cgroups and sandboxing primitives facilitates declarative service definitions that enforce resource limits and isolation policies automatically. This approach reduces manual configuration errors and allows system-wide uniform enforcement.

```
{
  "defaultAction": "SCMP_ACT_ERRNO",
  "syscalls": [
    {
      "names": ["read", "write", "exit", "exit_group"],
      "action": "SCMP_ACT_ALLOW"
    }
  ]
}
```

Preventing Resource Contention in Unpredictable Workloads

The unpredictable nature of modern workloads, composed of microservices, batch jobs, and interactive applications, demands dynamic and adaptive control. Monitoring tools integrated with cgroup statistics enable feedback loops that adjust resource limits based on observed contention and latency metrics. Reactive throttle mechanisms can temporarily reduce resource quotas for noisy workloads, mitigating cascading failures.

Resource overcommitment, while common, must be balanced with conservative enforcement of limits and rapid fault isolation through sandboxing to prevent systemic outages. Combining hierarchical cgroup organization and priority-based scheduling approximates service-level agreements by enforcing weighted fairness rather than strict partitioning.

The union of fine-grained resource control and sandboxing thus achieves a comprehensive governance framework, enabling systems to absorb high concurrency and workload volatility without compromising predictability, security, or throughput.

5.6. Scaling Bazel in Monorepos

Scaling Bazel to efficiently manage massive monorepos requires addressing architectural patterns that enable performant builds, avoiding common pitfalls, and implementing proven practices that mitigate the inherent complexity of large codebases. The enormous scale of monorepos-sometimes containing millions of source files and thousands of developers-imposes unique constraints on both Bazel's execution model and the underlying repository structure.

An effective directory layout is foundational to scalable Bazel builds. The layout must facilitate incremental builds, reduce dependency churn, and minimize the scope of affected targets whenever changes occur. A common architectural pattern is the *layered directory structure*, which organizes code by logical domains and feature boundaries, promoting encapsulation and clear dependency boundaries.

- **Vertical Slices:** Grouping files related to a single feature or service into cohesive vertical slices encapsulates the build dependencies. This limits the build and test scope to the relevant slice, reducing turnaround times.

- **Domain-Driven Grouping:** Organizing directories based on domain models (e.g., payments, user management) enables semantic import restrictions and clearly defined public APIs. Bazel rules can leverage these domain boundaries to enforce architectural constraints.

- **Third-Party Dependency Isolation:** External dependencies should be centralized under specific directories (e.g., third_party/) to avoid replication and to simplify dependency version management, ensuring consistency across the repo.

Ensuring that each directory corresponds to a well-scoped Bazel package (i.e., containing its own BUILD or BUILD.bazel file) is critical. Overly large packages with numerous targets result in extended build analysis phases and complicated dependency graphs, whereas excessively fine-grained packages increase overhead in managing build files.

In a massive monorepo, proper ownership assignment is essential to prevent bottlenecks and enable parallel development. Bazel itself is agnostic to code ownership, but integrating Bazel with code ownership models enhances build efficiency and code quality enforcement. The practice revolves around OWNER files, which explicitly specify responsible teams or individuals for each directory or package.

- **Hierarchical Ownership Inheritance:** OWNER files propagate downward through directory trees, allowing clear delegation of responsibility while avoiding duplication of ownership metadata.

- **Automated Ownership Verification:** By integrating OWNER metadata into continuous integration pipelines, permission checks can prevent unauthorized changes to critical build rule definitions or shared libraries, reducing build breakage.

- **Fine-Tuned Access Control:** OWNER files can assist in automatically triggering review workflows based on affected packages, ensuring that the right reviewers assess changes, which accelerates feedback cycles and stabilizes the build.

Bazel extensions and community tooling often provide utilities to parse these OWNER files and enforce ownership rules during the build and review processes.

Codebase sprawl in large monorepos manifests as uncontrolled inter-package dependencies, repository size growth, and prolonged build times. Strategies and Bazel features that directly mitigate these issues include:

Strict Dependency Enforcement

Bazel's `deps` attributes specify direct dependencies explicitly, enabling strict enforcement that prohibits undeclared dependencies from creeping into build targets. Introducing *aspect-based analysis* tools can automatically detect and disallow illegal transitive dependencies, keeping the dependency graph acyclic and manageable.

Repository Partitioning via `local_repository` and `remote_repository`

For extremely large codebases, logically partitioning parts of the repository into separate repositories or "subrepos" helps enforce build isolation and reduces the build graph's complexity per execution. Bazel's support for multiple repositories allows this with well-defined interfaces between subrepositories. However, over-partitioning leads to higher build orchestration costs and is a trade-off requiring deliberate architectural decisions.

Build File Generation and Maintenance Automation

Manually maintaining thousands of `BUILD` files becomes untenable at scale. Automated build file generation, either through internal tools or Bazel macros, enforces consistency and reduces human error. Key practices include:

- **Template-Based Macros:** Standardizing rules through macros reduces duplication and enforcement inconsistencies.

- **Code Generation for BUILD Files:** Tools scanning source code directories to produce or update Bazel build configurations ensure coverage without manual overhead.

Caching and Remote Execution Optimization

Remote caching and remote execution dramatically reduce build times by sharing artifacts and distributing build work across multiple machines. Large monorepos leverage these by:

- Ensuring *hermetic* builds to guarantee cache correctness.

- Partitioning build operations to maximize cache hits.

- Prioritizing remote execution for compute-intensive actions while minimizing network overhead.

Incremental and Selective Builds

Bazel supports fine-grained incremental builds by leveraging its dependency graph and file change detection. Ensuring the directory structure and dependencies reflect clear boundaries improves Bazel's ability to determine minimal rebuilds. Developers often use build query tools such as `bazel query` to analyze dependency impact and optimize the scope of build and test runs.

At the intersection of the above patterns, organizations emphasize continuous monitoring of build performance metrics and dependency health to proactively address scalability issues. Implementing *dependency hygiene policies*, coupled with tooling to visualize and audit the dependency graph, is instrumental in maintaining long-term build efficiency in monorepos.

Overall, scaling Bazel in monorepos demands a rigorous approach to directory architecture, clear ownership definitions through OWNER files, and systematic mechanisms for dependency and build file management. When applied coherently, these practices enable Bazel to harness its powerful incremental build capabilities even in the most expansive codebases, reducing developer turnaround time and improving CI stability.

5.7. Distributed Build Farms

Distributed build farms constitute the backbone of modern large-scale software development workflows, enabling efficient compilation, testing, and packaging across geographically dispersed resources. Their design and management demand meticulous orchestration, load balancing, error control, and observability strategies to ensure high availability and consistent performance at a global scale.

At the core of distributed build farms lies the principle of task decomposition and parallel execution. Build tasks, often represented as directed acyclic graphs (DAGs), are partitioned into discrete, independent units that can be executed concurrently on multiple worker nodes. This decomposition leverages spatial and temporal parallelism, significantly reducing the overall build latency compared to sequential local builds. A pivotal challenge emerges in orchestrating these tasks across heterogeneous and potentially unreliable resources, necessitating a robust orchestration layer.

Orchestration is typically handled by a centralized or federated scheduler that manages task assignment, dependency resolution, and resource allocation. The scheduler must maintain an up-to-date global view of the farm's state, encompassing available compute nodes, their workload, network latencies, and resource constraints. Effective orchestration involves dynamic scheduling algorithms that consider task priorities, estimated execution times, and historical performance metrics to optimize throughput and minimize resource contention.

Load balancing within distributed build farms is indispensable for maximizing resource utilization and preventing bottlenecks. Load balancing strategies can be adaptive or static. Static load balancing assigns tasks based on predefined rules or heuristics, such as consistent hashing functions or round-robin distributions. Adaptive load balancing, by contrast, relies on continuous monitoring and feedback loops, reallocating tasks in real time in response to fluctuations in node performance, network congestion, or task complexity. Algorithms such as least-loaded-node assignment or work-stealing are common approaches in adaptive balancing, promoting fairness and resilience.

Error handling in distributed build environments requires comprehensive fault detection, isolation, and recovery mechanisms. Given the scale and complexity, failures are inevitable-ranging from transient network disruptions and hardware malfunctions to software errors and data inconsistencies. Fault detection systems employ heartbeat protocols, log analysis, and exception handling frameworks to identify failures promptly. Once detected, fault isolation pinpoints the scope-whether a single build task, a worker node, or the coordinator itself. Recovery strategies include task re-execution on alternate nodes, checkpointing and rollback techniques, and redundancy through replication. Moreover, the orchestration layer must incorporate backoff policies and retry limits to avoid cascading failures and resource thrashing.

Observability enables operators to gain actionable insights into the state and performance of the build farm. A comprehensive observability stack integrates metrics, logs, and distributed tracing to provide end-to-end visibility. Metrics such as task queue lengths, node CPU and memory utilization, build success rates, and average latencies form quantitative indicators of system health. Log aggregation and analysis facilitate root cause diagnosis and anomaly detection, especially when combined with machine learning-based pattern recognition. Distributed tracing follows build task progress through various components, elucidating bottlenecks and interdependencies in real time. Centralized dashboards and alerting mechanisms allow rapid response to emerging issues, ensuring sustained operational reliability.

At a global scale, distributed build farms must also address challenges posed by geographical dispersion and multi-region deployment. Network latency and bandwidth variability impact task scheduling decisions, motivating locality-aware placement of build tasks to minimize cross-region communication. Data consistency models must balance strict transactional guarantees against practical eventual consistency to optimize storage and caching strategies. Federated orchestration frameworks leverage hierarchical control planes and regional coordinators to reduce centralization-induced latency and augment fault tolerance.

Security and access control form another vital aspect, particularly when build farms span multiple administrative domains or cloud providers. Authentication, authorization, and encryption protocols safeguard proprietary source code and build artifacts. Fine-grained role-based access control (RBAC) ensures that only authorized entities execute sensitive build operations. Additionally, secure software supply chain practices integrate integrity verification and provenance tracking into the distributed build process, mitigating risks from compromised dependencies or malicious modifications.

An illustrative orchestration pseudocode for task dispatching in a distributed build farm incorporates the described principles:

```
while build_queue not empty:
    task = build_queue.pop()
    candidate_nodes = get_available_nodes(task.requirements)
    if candidate_nodes is empty:
        wait_for_resources()
        continue
    target_node = select_least_loaded_node(candidate_nodes)
    try:
        dispatch_task(target_node, task)
    except DispatchError:
        retry_count = 0
        while retry_count < MAX_RETRIES:
            alternative_node = select_next_node(candidate_nodes,
    exclude=target_node)
            if alternative_node is None:
                log_error("No alternative nodes available.")
                break
            try:
                dispatch_task(alternative_node, task)
                break
            except DispatchError:
                retry_count += 1
        else:
            mark_task_failed(task)
```

This loop demonstrates critical facets: workload-aware node selection, error handling with retry logic, and fallback mechanisms in task assignment.

145

Managing distributed build farms at global scale entails integrating sophisticated orchestration, dynamic load balancing, resilient error management, and proactive observability. These components collectively establish a robust infrastructure capable of delivering rapid, reliable builds essential for continuous integration and deployment in complex software ecosystems.

Chapter 6

Testing with Bazel

Testing doesn't have to be slow, flaky, or unreliable—even in the biggest codebases. This chapter reveals how Bazel's test rules, rigorous isolation, and advanced caching create a testing experience that's both lightning fast and bulletproof. Discover techniques for everything from parallel test execution and sharding to CI integration, ensuring your builds deliver quality and confidence, every time.

6.1. Fundamental Testing Rules and Targets

Bazel provides a robust framework for declaring and executing tests through its built-in testing rules, which are designed to seamlessly integrate with various programming languages and environments. These rules encapsulate essential testing paradigms and automate the orchestration of test dependencies, execution environments, and result management. Understanding these rules, their corresponding test types, and the mechanics of target declarations is crucial for constructing scalable and maintainable test suites within Bazel workspaces.

The cornerstone of Bazel's testing infrastructure is the notion of a test rule, which is a first-class target type distinct from `cc_binary`, `java_binary`, or `py_binary` targets. Tests declared with `test` rules are intended to be executed by Bazel's test command `bazel test` and support features such as sandboxing, test sharding, timeout management, and cacheability of test results. Bazel includes built-in test rules for some of the core programming languages, each facilitating idiomatic ways to specify test sources, dependencies, and runtime configurations.

The primary built-in test rules include:

- `cc_test` for C and C++ codebases.

- `java_test` for Java projects.

- `py_test` for Python scripts and modules.

- `sh_test` for shell script-based tests.

These test rules extend their corresponding binary rules by adding test-specific parameters and conventions. For example, `cc_test` is akin to `cc_binary` but imposes expectations on test harness design, such as the use of frameworks like Google Test.

A typical test target declaration involves specifying the test rule, the source files constituting the test, and any necessary dependencies or data files required for execution. Consider the example of a `cc_test`:

```
cc_test(
    name = "math_utils_test",
    srcs = ["math_utils_test.cpp"],
    deps = [
        "//lib/math:math_utils",
        "@com_google_googletest//:gtest_main",
    ],
)
```

Here, the `math_utils_test` target compiles `math_utils_test.cpp` and links against the `math_utils` library as well as the external Google Test framework. When executed via `bazel test`, Bazel handles the compilation, execution in a sandboxed environment, and reporting of results following the Test Encyclopedia Format (XML), which is compatible with continuous integration systems.

Each language's test rule has conventions that align with the idiomatic testing frameworks and tooling of that language.

Java tests typically use `java_test` to declare JUnit or TestNG tests. The rule compiles the test classes, packages dependencies, and defines the JVM parameters for execution. Dependencies on the source code under test and testing frameworks must be explicitly declared.

```
java_test(
    name = "string_utils_test",
    srcs = glob(["src/test/java/**"]),
    deps = [
        "//src/main/java/com/example/stringutils",
        "@maven//:junit",
    ],
)
```

Python's `py_test` tests are expressed in interpreted scripts or modules, often leveraging `unittest` or `pytest`. Bazel ensures a hermetic environment with all declared dependencies present at test runtime.

```
py_test(
    name = "data_processor_test",
    srcs = ["data_processor_test.py"],
    deps = ["//lib/data:processor"],
)
```

`sh_test` executes shell scripts as tests and is useful for integration or end-to-end tests that require complex environment manipulations or orchestration outside traditional compiled languages.

```
sh_test(
    name = "deploy_integration_test",
    srcs = ["deploy_test.sh"],
    data = ["//config:prod_settings"],
)
```

Bazel provides two powerful commands beyond the basic test runs: `bazel run` and `bazel query`, which are instrumental in managing and organizing test suites effectively.

While `bazel test` is intended for running tests with full reporting, `bazel run` can execute test binaries or scripts interactively, bypassing some of the test harness features. This is useful for debugging or exploratory test execution:

```
bazel run //lib/math:math_utils_test
```

This command executes the compiled test target directly as a binary, allowing developers to see live output and debug interactively in cases where standard test reporting does not suffice.

The `bazel query` command enables introspection of the dependency graph and identification of test targets for complex builds. Combined with appropriate filters, it allows analysts or automation scripts to generate custom test suites dynamically.

For instance, to obtain all `cc_test` targets in the workspace, one would use:

```
bazel query 'kind("cc_test", //...)'
```

To find all tests depending on a particular library:

```
bazel query 'rdeps(//lib/math:math_utils, kind("test", //...))'
```

These queries can be combined with test execution commands to run subsets of tests pertinent to recent changes or code ownership regions, enabling sophisticated test orchestration workflows.

Bazel facilitates organizing tests into suites by defining alias targets or using `test_suite` rules, which group multiple test targets into logical collections without adding build overhead for a synthetic artifact. This abstraction permits the execution of coherent sets via one command:

```
test_suite(
    name = "all_math_tests",
    tests = [
        "//lib/math:math_utils_test",
        "//lib/math:geometry_test",
    ],
)
```

Executing bazel test //lib/math:all_math_tests will run all underlying tests in the suite, streamlining test management and reporting, especially in large codebases.

The architecture of Bazel's built-in testing rules, target declarations, and integrated tooling form a comprehensive ecosystem that supports rigorous test development and execution across languages and project scales. Mastery of these elements enables precision control over test workflows, optimized resource utilization, and robust CI/CD integration.

6.2. Test Execution Model and Isolation

Bazel's test execution paradigm is fundamentally anchored in its commitment to reproducibility and hermeticity, achieved primarily through sandboxing mechanisms. At its core, Bazel treats tests as build actions with strict input and output declarations, enabling rigorous control over their execution environments. This model ensures that tests run in isolated contexts, devoid of any unintended environmental influences or side effects, which is essential for deterministic outcomes and reliable continuous integration workflows.

Each test in Bazel is encapsulated within a sandbox that simulates a clean environment specifically tailored to the declared inputs of the test target. This sandboxing guarantees that tests cannot access files or system resources beyond those explicitly supplied, thereby nullifying potential interference from extraneous files, user environment variables, or background processes.

151

The isolation paradigm extends to the file system, network access, and even transparent system caches, making the sandbox an ephemeral, tightly constrained container for execution.

The lifecycle of a Bazel test run can be delineated into discrete stages:

1. **Preparation of the Execution Environment:** Before a test begins, Bazel analyzes the test target's declared inputs and outputs. All requisite dependencies—source files, generated artifacts, tools, and data—are materialized into a sandbox directory structure. This structure reflects a minimal, hermetically sealed file system namespace, exposing only those paths the test may legitimately access.

2. **Sandbox Initialization:** Bazel then initializes the sandbox, mapping declared inputs and fixed paths into the isolated directory. It typically leverages modern OS-level facilities such as `namespace` isolation on Linux, or filesystem virtualization techniques. This step also involves environment variable sanitization, where only a whitelisted set of variables (to guarantee essential runtime semantics) are inherited by the test process.

3. **Execution of the Test Action:** The test binary or script is executed within this constrained context. Since the sandbox lacks access to external state, any attempt by the test code to read files outside the declared inputs or write to disallowed locations results in execution failure or ignored side effects. Bazel monitors this execution closely, capturing standard output, error streams, and exit codes.

4. **Capturing and Validating Outputs:** Upon completion, Bazel collects the test's declared output files, ensuring that they exist and conform to expectations. It also archives logs and coverage data if applicable. The test action's exit status

is interpreted according to Bazel's rules: a zero exit code denotes success, nonzero denotes failure.

5. **Cleanup and Cache Management:** Finally, the sandbox environment is torn down. Bazel retains a cached representation of the executed test action, indexed by a fingerprint of its inputs and command-line arguments, enabling subsequent invocations with identical inputs to avoid redundant executions.

This isolation strategy rigorously enforces the *hermeticity* of test executions. No external dependencies—such as temporary files in user directories, network connections, or unrelated environment variables—can influence the test result. Consequently, identical test inputs and commands produce exactly the same outputs over any number of test runs, independent of the host developer machine or CI environment configuration.

Bazel also protects against hidden side effects frequently encountered in typical test workflows. For example, tests that modify global state, write to common temporary directories, or generate nondeterministic outputs are contained. Any such modification outside the sandbox boundaries is simply not reflected back into the build graph or workspace, preventing pollution of subsequent build or test runs. This containment eliminates a large class of flaky tests and nondeterministic failures, a significant improvement over traditional testing approaches that rely on implicit environmental assumptions.

Moreover, Bazel's test execution model integrates seamlessly with its caching and remote execution subsystems. Because overlays for the sandboxed environment and the fingerprints of inputs and commands are deterministic, test results can be stored and retrieved from local or remote caches. This capability significantly accelerates large-scale build and test pipelines by eliminating redundant test execution when inputs remain unchanged.

In some scenarios, tests require controlled access to network resources or longer-lived processes; Bazel accommodates such requirements through configurable sandboxing policies or by permitting explicit exemptions. Nevertheless, these deviations from strict isolation are carefully managed to maintain overall reproducibility guarantees.

The Bazel test execution model exemplifies a rigorous, sandboxed approach to testing, embedding isolation and hermeticity deeply into its lifecycle. By doing so, Bazel guarantees that test executions are repeatable, side-effect free, and immune to external environmental variance, forming a robust foundation for high-integrity software verification in complex, distributed development environments.

6.3. Parallel Test Execution and Sharding

Scaling software testing to meet the demands of modern, complex systems often requires distributing workloads across multiple processing units and machines. Parallel test execution and sharding represent two fundamental strategies that enable this distribution, significantly reducing overall test cycle time while maintaining or improving test coverage and reliability.

Parallel test execution involves running independent test cases simultaneously on different CPUs or cores within a single machine or across a cluster of machines. This approach exploits inherent test suite parallelism, assuming test cases do not have interdependencies or shared mutable state that would cause race conditions or nondeterministic behavior. Effective parallelization can decrease the elapsed wall-clock time for testing by a factor approaching the number of available execution units, subject to resource contention and overheads.

Test sharding extends this concept further by decomposing the

154

totality of tests into discrete subsets—or shards—that can be distributed across multiple nodes. Each shard contains a portion of the test suite, designed to be executed independently on a given environment with its own allocated computational resources. Sharding is particularly advantageous in continuous integration and delivery (CI/CD) pipelines where rapid feedback is critical and test suites are large or contain long-running tests.

Executing Tests in Parallel

There are several architectural considerations when enabling parallel execution on a single machine:

- **Test Independence:** Ensuring no stateful dependencies or shared resources between tests is paramount. Tests should be designed to be idempotent, deterministic, and isolated. Techniques such as database transaction rollbacks, mock services, and dedicated test data sets support this.

- **Resource Management:** CPU affinity, memory allocation, disk I/O, and network interface scheduling must be balanced. Overcommitting CPUs can lead to contention and performance degradation. Tools like process pools, thread pools, or container orchestration frameworks can enforce resource limits.

- **Test Runner Configuration:** Modern test frameworks provide flags or parameters to specify concurrency levels. For example, a command-line option such as `--jobs` or `--parallel` often controls the number of concurrent test executions, which should ideally correspond with the machine's logical cores.

Approaches to Test Sharding

Test sharding can be implemented using several strategies:

- **Static Partitioning:** The test suite is divided into equally sized shards based on a fixed criterion such as test file names or alphabetical test case grouping. While straightforward, this can lead to unbalanced execution times if tests are uneven in duration or complexity.

- **Dynamic Partitioning:** Shards are generated based on historical runtime data, distributing tests to equalize execution time per shard. This requires maintaining accurate timing artifacts from previous runs and recomputing shards periodically.

- **Hash-Based Partitioning:** Tests are assigned to shards using a hash function on test identifiers. This yields deterministic shard allocation which facilitates caching and incremental execution, though it may not perfectly balance load.

For example, a simple static sharding based on test file count might look like:

```
# Assume 100 test files, shard count = 4
shard_id=$1  # Shard index from CI job configuration, 0 to 3
total_shards=4
all_tests=( $(find tests/ -name '*_test.py' | sort) )
shard_tests=()

for ((i=0; i < ${#all_tests[@]}; i++)); do
  if (( i % total_shards == shard_id )); then
    shard_tests+=("${all_tests[i]}")
  fi
done

# Run tests in the shard
pytest "${shard_tests[@]}"
```

Infrastructure Considerations

Distributing shards across multiple nodes requires coordination, which can be facilitated by CI/CD systems such as Jenkins, GitLab CI, or CircleCI. These platforms enable matrix or parallel job configurations, allocating resources dynamically and aggregating results at the end of execution.

When tests are executed in heterogeneous environments or containers, ensuring uniform test environments is essential to prevent variability in results. Containerization tools like Docker or orchestration systems such as Kubernetes can standardize the runtime environment. Network-based shared storage or artifact repositories enable centralized access to test binaries, baselines, and results.

Best Practices for Configuration

- **Granularity Control:** Tests should be small enough to allow efficient parallelization, but large enough to amortize overhead from startup and initialization costs. Grouping micro-tests that have common setup dependencies into single shards can improve throughput.

- **Balancing and Load Estimation:** Employ runtime metrics and historical execution statistics to balance test shards. Overloaded shards cause straggler tests that dominate total runtime, negating parallel speed gains.

- **Environment Isolation:** Each parallel test execution or shard should run in a sandboxed environment, avoiding conflicts over files, databases, network ports, or other shared resources.

- **Robust Failure Handling:** Parallel runs can obfuscate failure detection. Implement mechanisms for detailed logging, unique output files per shard, and consistent exit codes to facilitate debugging and retries.

- **Resource Limits and Quotas:** Enforce upper bounds on memory, CPU, and I/O bandwidth per parallel test or shard to prevent overall system thrashing.

Common Pitfalls and Mitigations

- **Flaky Tests Amplification:** Tests with intermittent failures become more problematic in parallel settings due to increased concurrency. Root cause analysis and stabilization of flaky tests is vital before enabling large-scale parallelism.

- **Hidden Dependencies:** Tests relying on global state, environment variables, or singleton services may pass sequentially but fail unpredictably in parallel. Comprehensive isolation and mocking mitigate these issues.

- **Overhead Overshadowing Gains:** Excessive coordination, environment setup, or artifacts transfer can consume more time than the parallel execution saves. Design pipelines to reuse cached environments and minimize data transfer.

- **Non-Deterministic Test Order:** Tests that rely implicitly on a fixed execution order may produce inconsistent results. Tests must be order-independent to leverage parallelism safely.

Parallel test execution and sharding are indispensable techniques for accelerating test runs and increasing feedback velocity in modern development workflows. Successful implementation requires a confluence of test design discipline, infrastructure planning, and thoughtful configuration. When applied correctly, these approaches enable scalable, resilient, and maintainable testing architectures capable of keeping pace with continuous delivery imperatives.

6.4. Test Caching, Flakiness, and Reliability

Bazel's test execution framework integrates a sophisticated caching mechanism designed to optimize the trade-off between accuracy and speed. By caching test results, Bazel avoids redundant re-execution of tests when the inputs remain unchanged, significantly accelerating iterative development cycles. This mechanism hinges upon content-addressable storage whereby the cache keys encode the precise combination of test inputs, including source files, dependencies, build flags, and environment variables. Only when these inputs differ does Bazel deem the test outcome stale, triggering a new execution phase. This deterministic approach ensures correctness by tightly coupling cache validity to the exact test context, rather than relying on timestamps or heuristic invalidation.

The core of Bazel's caching strategy relies on hashing the declared test inputs along with their complete transitive closure. This includes explicit file dependencies, generated artifacts, and environmental factors necessary for reproducible test runs. Tests failing to declare these dependencies properly risk cache misses or, more perniciously, invalid cache hits yielding erroneous results. Explicitly accounting for test inputs prevents false positives in cache retrieval and reinforces the hermeticity of the build and test execution.

Aggressive mitigation of test flakiness is essential for reliable continuous integration workflows. Flaky tests manifest when results vary nondeterministically due to unresolved external state, timing dependencies, or resource contention. Bazel facilitates robust test isolation to minimize flakiness by enforcing sandboxed test execution environments. These environments restrict file system access, isolate network interactions, and normalize runtime conditions to create reproducible and stable test invocations. The sandbox also clamps resource usage such as CPU and memory to circumvent intermittent failures linked to system load variability.

To further combat flakiness, Bazel encourages deterministic test design principles. This includes avoiding reliance on external systems such as databases or remote services, which inject latency and unpredictability. Environment-dependent logic should be ab-

stracted behind injected mocks or stubs to ensure consistent behavior regardless of execution context. Tests exhibiting nondeterministic behavior should be instrumented with thorough logging
and deterministic seeds for pseudorandom processes.

When flakiness persists, Bazel's diagnostic tooling becomes indispensable. The test log output, accessible through Bazel's queryable
interface, provides granular insights into test invocation parameters, environment snapshots, and intermediate states. Tests can
be rerun with increased verbosity or in a remote-debugging mode
to capture elusive race conditions or resource deadlocks. Additionally, Bazel supports repeated test invocations controlled by the
--flaky_test_attempts flag, enabling empirical measurement of
flakiness rates. These repeated executions reveal sporadic failures
by accumulating multiple test outcomes in a single execution cycle.

```
bazel test //my/package:my_flaky_test --flaky_test_attempts=5
```

```
INFO: Running 5 attempts for //my/package:my_flaky_test because flaky test is
  enabled.
Attempt 1: PASSED
Attempt 2: FAILED
Attempt 3: PASSED
Attempt 4: PASSED
Attempt 5: FAILED
```

Analyzing such execution patterns aids in isolating non-
deterministic dependencies. Following identification, flaky tests
often undergo refactoring or are segregated into dedicated suites
to prevent undue noise in mainline builds. Bazel additionally
permits marking tests as flaky through metadata, enabling
selective rerun strategies while maintaining overall test suite
efficiency.

Stabilization of tests also relies on continuous monitoring and quality control integration. Bazel's event stream API exposes real-time
test status, execution times, and cache hit rates. These metrics feed
into dashboards and alerts that flag anomalous behavior trends.
Persistently flaky or underperforming tests can be prioritized for

developer attention, ensuring the collective health of the codebase. Automated detection of regression in test reliability complements rigorous manual debugging, establishing a feedback loop that preserves long-term test integrity.

Moreover, test result caching and flakiness control are intrinsically linked. Excessive flakiness erodes confidence in cached results, often necessitating cache invalidation or forced re-execution, which negates the performance benefits. Bazel's nuanced cache management includes configurable policies to handle flaky tests, such as retry thresholds and fallback to cache misses upon suspected instability. This intelligent interplay balances correctness with efficiency, adapting to evolving project complexity.

In sum, Bazel's approach to test caching intertwined with proactive flakiness elimination forms the foundation of a reliable and performant testing ecosystem. Hermetic test inputs, sandbox-enforced isolation, and rigorous diagnostic instrumentation collectively reduce nondeterminism. Coupled with monitoring infrastructure to detect and remediate instability, these mechanisms sustain high-confidence, repeatable test outcomes essential for large-scale software development.

6.5. Coverage Analysis and Quality Metrics

Coverage analysis is an essential aspect of maintaining and improving software quality, allowing development teams to quantify how well their tests exercise the codebase. Within the realm of Bazel-a build and test tool known for its high performance and correctness guarantees-integrating coverage tools requires careful configuration and an understanding of Bazel's action graph to ensure accurate and actionable results.

Bazel supports coverage instrumentation primarily through its built-in support for language-specific coverage flags and its integration with external coverage tools such as lcov and gcov for C/C++ and Java. Coverage data is gathered by running instrumented tests and then processed into reports that highlight which lines, functions, or branches of code have executed during testing. This process starts with the configuration of the build targets to enable coverage instrumentation.

To enable coverage collection in Bazel, the --collect_coverage flag is used alongside bazel test, specifying that the tests not only run but also gather coverage data:

```
bazel test //path/to:target --collect_coverage --
    coverage_report_generator=lcov
```

Here, the coverage_report_generator option instructs Bazel which tool to use for merging and generating the coverage output. Using lcov generates a coverage.info file, which conforms to a widely-supported format for coverage visualization and further analysis.

Coverage data retrieval in Bazel leverages the _coverage_output directory created post-test execution. Within this directory, the raw coverage artifacts produced by the instrumentation are collected. Bazel's coverage support is tightly coupled with its test cache and dependency graph, ensuring coverage information is only rebuilt and recomputed when underlying source or test artifacts change. This paradigm enhances efficiency while preserving data accuracy.

To transform raw data into actionable information, developers frequently use coverage report tools such as genhtml for lcov, which produce interactive HTML reports illustrating the coverage status at line and branch granularity. Such detailed views enable developers to identify untested sections precisely and optimize test suites accordingly.

The essential dimensions inspected in coverage reports include:

- **Line coverage**: Percentage of executable lines exercised.

- **Branch coverage**: Percentage of possible branches (e.g., `if/else` paths) tested.

- **Function coverage**: Fraction of defined functions invoked during tests.

Quantitative metrics drawn from these dimensions serve as key indicators of test effectiveness and software reliability.

Advanced integration scenarios in Bazel enable automation of quality gates based on coverage thresholds. Bazel's extensible build rules and its Starlark scripting language allow embedding coverage analysis into the build pipeline. Coverage summary files can be parsed post-test execution to assert minimum coverage percentages. If these thresholds are not met, the build can be configured to fail, thereby enforcing quality contracts.

A typical coverage enforcement strategy involves:

- Collect coverage data using Bazel's `--collect_coverage` option.

- Use a custom Starlark rule or external script to parse the coverage summary file.

- Compare the coverage metrics against predetermined thresholds.

- Fail the build step or generate warnings if metrics fall below acceptable levels.

The following example illustrates a simplified shell script checking line coverage from an `lcov` report:

```
#!/bin/bash
COVERAGE_INFO="coverage/coverage.info"
MIN_COVERAGE=80
```

```
line_coverage=$(lcov --summary $COVERAGE_INFO | grep lines | awk
    '{print $2}' | tr -d '%')

if (( $(echo "$line_coverage < $MIN_COVERAGE" | bc -l) )); then
    echo "Error: Line coverage $line_coverage% is below threshold
      of $MIN_COVERAGE%."
    exit 1
else
    echo "Coverage check passed: $line_coverage% >= $MIN_COVERAGE
      %"
fi
```

This script can be integrated as part of a `bazel_run_local` target or invoked in a CI/CD pipeline stage, enforcing coverage discipline continuously.

Beyond line coverage, Bazel's extensibility allows integration with sophisticated quality metric tools such as SonarQube or Codecov by exporting coverage reports in compatible formats. These integrations enable cross-referencing of test coverage with static analysis findings, code complexity, or duplication metrics, providing a more comprehensive perspective on overall code health.

A critical consideration when working with Bazel's coverage capabilities in large-scale monorepos or polyglot projects is ensuring consistent instrumentation across languages and build configurations. Bazel's rule ecosystem addresses these challenges by providing unified interfaces and configurations for toolchain providers, thus abstracting platform-specific nuances. For example, the `java_test` and `cc_test` rules support coverage flags and action metadata uniformly to simplify cross-language coverage aggregation.

Sometimes, coverage artifacts can balloon in size, especially in extensive codebases with numerous tests. Bazel supports partial coverage collection and filtering through target specifications and exclusion lists. Selective instrumentation reduces overhead and focuses attention on high-priority components. Developers can specify inclusion or exclusion patterns by customizing coverage attributes in Bazel build definitions; for example, excluding generated files or third-party dependencies.

Continuous monitoring of coverage metrics over time is instrumental for preventing test erosion and technical debt. By integrating Bazel test runs with coverage enforcement into CI pipelines, incremental drops in coverage can be detected early, triggering alerts or rollback actions. Coupled with code review policies requiring coverage increases or retention, this practice fosters sustained test quality.

Bazel's integration of coverage tools empowers teams to achieve granular visibility into test effectiveness, derive actionable insights, and enforce rigorous quality metrics automatically for every build. This tight coupling of build correctness, test automation, and coverage analysis under a unified framework reduces overhead, eliminates manual errors, and fosters a culture of quality-driven software engineering.

6.6. Continuous Integration with Bazel

Bazel's design philosophy aligns with the demands of modern Continuous Integration and Continuous Deployment systems. Its capabilities for incremental builds, hermetic execution, and fine-grained dependency analysis enable scalable automation of builds and tests within developer workflows and production pipelines. Integrating Bazel into CI/CD requires careful configuration and patterns that leverage its strengths while addressing the needs of automated environments.

Central to effective integration is hermeticity. Bazel ensures builds are fully reproducible by encapsulating all inputs and outputs, minimizing environmental discrepancies that often hinder CI reliability. This reproducibility is particularly advantageous in distributed configurations where build agents may differ in software and hardware. When invoking Bazel in CI pipelines, pin the workspace state with explicit declarations in WORKSPACE and BUILD files, and use tagged dependencies reflecting committed versions of external repositories. Enabling remote caching and remote execution further enhances scalability, permitting multiple agents to share build artifacts and distribute workloads efficiently.

The mandatory starting point in a Bazel-based pipeline is to invoke the `bazel build` and `bazel test` commands on the target set representing the full verification scope. A typical invocation in a shell context follows:

```
bazel test //...
```

This command directs Bazel to test all targets recursively from the root package. To optimize performance, specify test filters or tags to restrict the scope dynamically. For example, when only unit tests are necessary, target tests with specific tags:

```
bazel test --test_tag_filters=unit //...
```

Bazel's ability to run tests in parallel, governed by the `--jobs` flag, is crucial for reducing CI runtime. Calibrate parallelism based on available CPU and memory resources on CI agents to avoid contention and flakiness.

Configuration management within CI systems must handle Bazel flags and environment settings systematically. CI scripts commonly maintain a `.bazelrc` file tailored for the pipeline environment, which may include flags such as:

```
# .bazelci.bazelrc
build --remote_cache=https://bazel-cache.example.com
build --remote_upload_local_results=true
build --experimental_strict_action_env
test --test_output=errors
test --flaky_test_attempts=3
```

These settings enable remote caching to speed up builds, enforce strict environment variables to guard against nondeterminism, and configure test-retry mechanisms that reduce transient failures affecting pipeline stability.

Integration with popular CI platforms-Jenkins, GitHub Actions, GitLab CI and Buildkite-requires orchestrating Bazel commands, caching layers, and output reporting. Each platform supports distinct mechanisms for artifact storage and test-result parsing. Bazel emits JUnit-compatible XML reports by default, compatible with most CI test-report aggregation systems. Pipelines should capture the Bazel output directory (`bazel-testlogs`) as an artifact to preserve test logs for later inspection.

Caching is a fundamental lever for improving pipeline efficiency. Local cache directories, usually `$HOME/.cache/bazel`, can be preserved between job executions on dedicated agents or ephemeral containers. More effectively, remote caching servers prevent redundant compilations across distributed agents. A typical remote-caching setup depends on a gRPC or HTTP cache service configured in the Bazelrc file.

A minimal remote-caching model in CI is expressed as:

```
bazel build --remote_cache=http://cache.ci.internal:8080 //...
```

For environments demanding greater scale, Bazel supports **remote execution**, distributing build actions across a cluster of workers. Remote execution differs from caching in that it offloads the actual compilation and test runs, potentially reducing agent workload and build duration drastically, albeit requiring more complex infrastructure.

To accommodate monorepos with thousands of targets and extensive test sets, pipelines adopt a test-sharding pattern. Bazel supports sharding natively via the `--test_sharding_strategy=explicit` flag, enabling parallel execution of subdivided test subsets:

```
bazel test //... --test_sharding_strategy=explicit --test_arg=--
    shard_count=5 --test_arg=--shard_index=0
```

This command runs the first shard (index 0) of five shards, allowing parallel CI jobs to execute different subsets independently and accelerate overall testing.

Maintaining fast feedback cycles relies on incremental builds and tests triggered by precise change detection. Bazel's query language and aspect system can identify affected targets based on changed files, enabling selective build and test runs. For instance, a pipeline may first detect changed targets using:

```
bazel query "rdeps(//..., set($(git diff --name-only HEAD~1)))"
```

Subsequently, the pipeline builds and tests only those targets, conserving resources and providing rapid validation suited to iterative development.

Adopting Bazel in a CI/CD context requires ongoing attention to workspace consistency, cache hygiene, and tuning build and test concurrency aligned with infrastructure resources. When orchestrated correctly, Bazel fosters a highly deterministic, scalable, and performant automation environment supporting rapid developer feedback and reliable production delivery.

6.7. Advanced Test Rule Development

Custom test rule development with Starlark in build systems such as Bazel involves creating specialized, efficient, and reusable testing logic that addresses complex, domain-specific requirements. Beyond basic test definitions, advanced test rule development emphasizes abstraction, parameterization and the balance between flexibility and maintainability to support scalable test architectures.

1. Abstraction Through Function Decomposition

Complex test rules benefit from isolating components such as command-line construction, test environment setup and output validation into dedicated helper functions. This decomposition simplifies reasoning about each part and facilitates modifications without unintended side effects. For example, separating the logic that builds the test executable command from the logic that computes environment variables prevents entanglement and enhances clarity.

2. Parameterization for Flexibility

Parameterization enables a single test rule to support varied behaviors across different testing scenarios. Typical parameters include:

- `srcs`: source files or scripts executed during the test.

- `deps`: dependencies required to compile or run the test.

- `data`: auxiliary files important for runtime inputs.

- `env`: environment variables customized per test instance.

- `args`: command-line arguments passed to the test binary.

- `timeout`: constraints on the test execution time.

- `tags`: metadata to categorize or filter tests.

Explicit parameter declarations with default values enable consumers of the rule to override behavior easily while maintaining a consistent interface.

3. Statelessness and Incrementality

To integrate seamlessly with incremental build and test systems, custom test rules must avoid side effects in their Starlark implementation. Computation in rule implementations should be deterministic and based solely on declared inputs. Avoiding external state ensures that the build system's caching and change detection mechanisms work optimally.

4. Utilization of Provider Abstractions

Providers in Starlark encapsulate information passed between rules. When designing custom test rules, defining and consuming

169

providers enables the capture of rich metadata-such as test results, coverage data and diagnostics-for efficient downstream processing. For example, a test rule might export a `TestInfo` provider carrying result summaries or artifacts.

5. Execution Wrapper with Starlark Executable

Custom tests often require runtime scaffolding-launching a sandboxed environment, setting up network mocks or collecting logs. Employing Starlark `executable` objects as wrappers around test binaries provides a flexible hook for advanced orchestration without external scripts. This approach keeps test runtime logic within the build system.

6. Best Practices for Reusable Test Rule Libraries

- Modular Rule Design: build small, composable rules rather than monolithic ones to enable reuse in diverse settings.

- Clear Documentation: document parameters and expected behavior explicitly to reduce misuse.

- Metadata Propagation: ensure test results, tags and environment information propagate through providers for filtering, scheduling and reporting.

- Consistent Naming Conventions: employ uniform attribute and target naming to enhance discoverability and maintainability.

- Use of `attr` and Implicit Outputs: define outputs and inputs declaratively with `attr` declarations and implicit outputs to leverage Bazel's caching and change detection automatically.

Illustrative Example: Parameterized Starlark Test Rule

The following snippet demonstrates a parameterized test rule that abstracts command construction and environment setup. It accepts arbitrary arguments and environment variables while producing a test target with appropriate outputs.

```
def _custom_test_impl(ctx):
    # Build the command line by combining test binary and args
    test_cmd = [ctx.executable._test_binary.path] + ctx.attr.args

    # Prepare environment variables dict for execution
    env = dict(ctx.attr.env)
    env["RUN_ID"] = ctx.label.name

    # Define the TestInfo provider with metadata
    test_info = struct(
        test_executable = ctx.executable._test_binary,
        timeout = ctx.attr.timeout,
        tags = ctx.attr.tags,
    )

    # Return default test target with TestInfo provider
    return [
        DefaultInfo(files = depset([ctx.executable._test_binary])
        ),
        test_info,
        # The run action is implied when executable attribute is
    set
    ]

custom_test = rule(
    implementation = _custom_test_impl,
    attrs = {
        "_test_binary": attr.label(executable=True, mandatory=
    True),
        "args":             attr.string_list(default=[]),
        "env":              attr.string_dict(default={}),
        "timeout":          attr.int(default=300),
        "tags":             attr.string_list(default=[]),
    },
    test = True,
)
```

In this example, the attribute _test_binary expects a binary executable that performs the test. The args and env parameters allow dynamic customization, while the timeout and tags attributes integrate with the broader testing infrastructure for resource and metadata management.

Performance Considerations

High-performance custom test rules depend on minimizing unnecessary actions and leveraging artifact caching. Declaring precise

inputs and outputs, combined with thorough use of depset structures for file collections, avoids redundant rebuilds. Explicit environment variable declarations enable deterministic test environments, preventing flaky failures. Parallelism can be exposed by
designing rules that avoid shared state and minimize inter-target
dependencies.

Extending Test Rules with Custom Execution Strategies

For specialized runtime conditions-such as hardware-in-the-loop
testing, distributed test harnesses or fuzzing campaigns-Starlark
custom test rules can invoke external orchestrators through
ctx.actions.run or ctx.actions.run_shell. These invocations
offer fine-grained control over inputs, arguments, environment
variables and expected outputs. Wrapping such workflows
as standard test targets integrates exotic scenarios into the
unified build and test ecosystem without sacrificing control or
performance.

Mastering advanced test rule development in Starlark is essential
for building resilient, scalable and maintainable automated testing
workflows that adapt efficiently to evolving technical and organizational requirements. By embracing abstraction, parameterization,
deterministic, side-effect-free implementations and rich metadata
propagation, developers unlock the full potential of the build system's incremental execution engines while ensuring test logic remains clear, reusable and high-performing.

Chapter 7

Security, Compliance, and Reproducibility

In today's software landscape, build integrity is your first and last line of defense. This chapter unpacks how Bazel empowers teams to achieve airtight reproducibility, harden their build pipelines, and automate compliance—without compromising speed. From cryptographic build attestation to sandboxing and dependency audits, discover the state-of-the-art practices that help safeguard engineering velocity and your organization's reputation.

7.1. Hermetic Builds and Supply Chain Security

Hermetic builds are a foundational concept in modern software engineering, providing a disciplined approach to achieve reproducibility, provenance, and defense against supply chain attacks. Bazel's design philosophy explicitly embraces hermeticity to ensure that build outputs depend exclusively on declared inputs, that environments are strictly controlled, and that side effects are elim-inated. This section elucidates how Bazel's hermetic principles ful-fill these objectives and delineates best practices that organizations can adopt to fortify software supply chains.

At its core, hermeticity in Bazel is achieved by enforcing com-plete specification and isolation of build inputs and environments. Each build step in Bazel executes within a sandbox that restricts access to the file system and network, allowing only declared in-puts and tools. This isolation guarantees that no undeclared, tran-sient, or external state can influence the build outputs, thereby en-abling reproducible builds. By eliminating implicit dependencies-such as system-wide libraries, environment variables, or network resources-hermetic builds ensure that identical inputs and build configurations produce bitwise-identical artifacts irrespective of the host system or time of build.

Reproducibility is a critical defense against supply chain attacks. If a binary is reproducible, any unauthorized modification to source code, dependencies, or build processes can be detected by compar-ing the resulting build artifact with a known good version. Bazel achieves reproducibility through several mechanisms: content-addressable storage of input files, strict sandboxing, and deter-ministic rule implementations. Inputs and intermediate artifacts are tracked via cryptographic hashes, ensuring traceable prove-nance for every build output. Deterministic rule definitions further guarantee that build steps yield consistent results, avoiding factors such as timestamp embedding or nondeterministic file ordering.

To maintain provenance and traceability, Bazel integrates meta-data recording and artifact hashing throughout the build graph. All dependencies-source files, tools, and external repositories-are explicitly declared as inputs, and their content digests are in-corporated into the build graph's state. This metadata facili-tates verification chains where any discrepancy in inputs or in-termediate results triggers a rebuild or alerts to potential tam-

pering. Moreover, Bazel's external repositories mechanism leverages content-addressable identifiers, for example, commit SHAs or
cryptographic hashes, ensuring that dependencies are immutable
and auditable. Supply chain security efforts are bolstered by automating these provenance guarantees to minimize human error
and enhance transparency.

Isolation from untrusted artifacts is paramount in preventing contamination of the build pipeline. Bazel's sandboxing capability
leverages operating system primitives-such as Linux namespaces
and seccomp filters-to physically segregate build actions. This isolation restricts network access and controls the file system namespace accessible to each action, effectively quarantining untrusted
inputs from core build processes. For example, when integrating third-party dependencies or tools, sandbox constraints prevent
them from interacting with the local environment or reading unauthorized files. This containment significantly reduces the attack
surface for malicious payloads or compromised binaries attempt-
ing to pivot within the build host.

Best practices to complement Bazel's hermetic approach encompass rigorous dependency management, secure fetching of external repositories, and preventive auditing. Organizations should
consider the following guidelines:

- Pin dependencies by immutable references (e.g., specific
  commit hashes) to ensure consistency.

- Verify cryptographic signatures to protect against unverified
  or malicious code injection.

- Leverage cryptographic verification tools and reproducibility
  testing to detect unauthorized changes proactively.

- Enforce sandboxed builds consistently within continuous integration pipelines, rejecting any artifacts built without declared dependencies or with excessive privileges.

- Design custom Bazel rules to adhere strictly to hermetic principles, avoiding undeclared inputs and nondeterministic behaviors to maintain overall build integrity.

Another critical practice is the avoidance of network dependencies during build execution whenever feasible. Network access introduces variability and security risks, including reliance on potentially compromised package repositories or man-in-the-middle attacks. To mitigate such risks, Bazel supports local caching of remote repositories and artifacts, enabling builds to occur in completely offline and deterministic environments once dependencies are fetched and verified. Combined with sandboxed execution, this approach prevents runtime injection or modification of build inputs.

Bazel's hermetic build system embodies a comprehensive strategy for supply chain security. It leverages process isolation, precise input specification, and rigorous provenance tracking. Reproducibility establishes a verifiable chain of custody for software artifacts, while sandboxing materially limits attack vectors within the build environment. By adhering to best practices-such as explicit dependency pinning, cryptographic validation, and sandbox enforcement-development teams can robustly defend their build pipelines against supply chain compromise, ensuring integrity and trustworthiness of software delivered to production.

7.2. Sandboxing and Attack Surface Minimization

Bazel's sandboxing mechanisms constitute a foundational pillar in ensuring secure, hermetic builds and tests. Sandboxing confines build actions within isolated environments, restricting their interaction with the host system to reduce the attack surface significantly. This containment is crucial to prevent unintentional dependencies, manipulation of external artifacts, and unauthorized data access during the build lifecycle.

The essence of Bazel's sandboxing lies in its deterministic and minimal execution environment. Each build action runs in a dedicated sandbox, a transient directory structured to expose only the declared inputs and outputs. The sandbox enforces a strict file system boundary, denying all filesystem operations outside this scope unless explicitly permitted. This containment not only prevents leakage of sensitive system resources but also mitigates the risk of persistent side effects that can compromise system integrity or leak confidential build information.

Bazel's sandboxing policies extend beyond simple directory restrictions through configurable sandbox strategies. Common strategies include the use of Linux namespaces, chroot environments, and Linux Security Modules (LSMs) like SELinux or AppArmor, depending on platform capabilities and administrator preferences. For instance, the Linux sandbox strategy leverages user namespaces and seccomp filters to curtail system calls available to build actions, reducing kernel-level attack vectors. Advanced sandbox policies allow fine-tuning of permitted behaviors, balancing strict isolation with necessary functionality such as network access or specialized device interaction.

An essential feature of Bazel's sandbox environment is environment lockdown. By default, Bazel sanitizes and controls environment variables visible to sandboxed processes to prevent uncontrolled environmental influence. Common environment variables like PATH, HOME, and locale settings are explicitly set, ensuring reproducible environments and minimizing the risk of injecting malicious configurations or dynamic loading of untrusted code. This environmental hermeticity hinders attackers from exploiting environment-based weaknesses or loading unintended shared libraries.

In some advanced scenarios, additional environment lockdown

can be achieved through Bazel's support for portable sandbox configurations. These configurations can specify exact environment contents, additional mounts, and bind-mount restrictions, further restricting potential side channels or covert data exfiltration paths. For example, sandbox policies can exclude network access entirely by unmounting network devices or by applying network namespaces that isolate the build action network stack. Restricting network access limits the opportunity for sandboxed actions to communicate with external servers, which could be exploited to leak sensitive build information or introduce malicious payloads.

Audit-readiness is a critical consideration for organizations with rigorous compliance and security requirements. Bazel facilitates audit-readiness through comprehensive sandbox logging and metadata collection. Every sandboxed build action logs filesystem operations, environmental variables, and system calls, which can be aggregated for forensic analysis or regulatory auditing. This logging provides detailed traceability that is indispensable for incident response, enabling rapid identification of anomalous behavior or security policy violations.

To illustrate Bazel sandbox usage and customization, consider the following command line snippet invoking Bazel with a custom sandbox configuration that disables network access and sets a controlled environment:

```
bazel build //myproject:target \
  --sandbox_fake_hostname=localhost \
  --sandbox_additional_network_namespace=false \
  --sandbox_debug \
  --sandbox_use_fake_hostname \
  --sandbox_fake_username=user \
  --sandbox_tmpfs_path=/tmp \
  --sandbox_writable_path=/dev/null
```

These flags instruct Bazel to replace the host network access with a fake hostname, disable networking within the sandbox network namespace, and provide debug information to inspect sandbox actions. By restricting writable paths and controlling temporary directories, it further reduces the sandbox's attack surface.

The resulting build logs will be rich with sandbox audit data, simplified here:

```
INFO: Running sandboxed build for //myproject:target
DEBUG: Sandbox PID 12345 started
DEBUG: Mounted inputs: /workspace/myproject/src, /toolchain/bin
DEBUG: Applied seccomp filter: Blocked syscall write to /etc/passwd
DEBUG: Network namespace isolated: no external connectivity
DEBUG: Sandbox PID 12345 exited successfully
```

This detailed capture ensures transparency and facilitates post-mortem reviews of suspicious or unauthorized build actions.

In summary, Bazel's sandboxing architecture—through a combination of filesystem isolation, namespace containment, environment lockdown, and comprehensive auditing—provides a robust framework for minimizing the attack surface inherent to build and test processes. These design choices are instrumental in reducing risk exposure while maintaining the flexibility and performance crucial to large-scale builds. Harnessing these capabilities properly aligns with security best practices, enabling organizations to sustain trust in their software supply chain integrity.

7.3. Dependency Auditing and Licenses

Automated dependency analysis is an essential practice in contemporary software development, particularly within Bazel-based build systems where reproducibility and hermeticity are paramount. Bazel's fine-grained build rules and explicit dependency declarations facilitate precise control over external libraries and components. However, ensuring license compliance and vulnerability management requires integrating specialized tooling that complements Bazel's native capabilities.

Dependency auditing begins with the ability to accurately extract and catalog all external dependencies, including transient transitive dependencies. Bazel's `repository_rule` abstractions and external workspace definitions enable controlled inclusion of third-party artifacts, but this alone does not guarantee awareness of the license obligations or security posture of those dependencies. Automated tools designed to parse Bazel workspace configurations and analyze dependency graphs fill this gap. These tools typically perform static analysis on Bazel's workspace files and BUILD targets, recursively identifying dependency metadata such as version numbers, source locations, and associated licenses.

A critical component of such auditing systems is the creation of a comprehensive Software Bill of Materials (SBOM). The SBOM provides an exhaustive inventory of all components, their origins, and respective license declarations. Ensuring the SBOM's accuracy and currency is fundamental, particularly for organizations subjected to regulatory scrutiny or employing rigorous open source governance policies. Automated SBOM generation tools integrated into Bazel workflows leverage Bazel's query capabilities (for example, `bazel query 'deps(//path/to:target)'`) to enumerate all dependencies systematically, thereby enabling downstream compliance verification.

License compliance workflows built around Bazel must accommodate the diversity of license types, be they permissive, copyleft, or proprietary. Automated license scanners analyze the contents of dependencies and cross-reference license identifiers against organizational policies. Integration at the build-system level enables early detection of license conflicts or unsupported licenses before artifacts are produced or released. Typical policy enforcement includes:

- Blocking or flagging dependencies that violate corporate licensing policies.

- Generating compliance reports to be submitted with software releases.

- Automating notices and attribution generation required by certain open source licenses.

To implement these workflows effectively, continuous integration (CI) pipelines employing Bazel often incorporate dedicated license scanning steps. These steps invoke tools capable of parsing Bazel-generated SBOMs or intermediate representations and perform license verification automatically. When a policy violation is detected, the pipeline can trigger alerts or halt the build process, thus preventing non-compliant artifacts from progressing through the software lifecycle.

Equally important is incorporating vulnerability scanners into Bazel-based environments to detect and mitigate security risks originating from third-party dependencies. Vulnerability scanners operate by correlating dependency metadata against databases of known security advisories, such as the National Vulnerability Database (NVD) or vendor-specific feeds. Integrating these scanners into Bazel builds requires mechanisms to extract dependency versions accurately and provide them to scanning tools, either through generated SBOM files or via API interactions.

A representative workflow consists of the following steps:

- Execute a Bazel query command to obtain a complete, reproducible list of dependencies for the build target.

- Generate an SBOM in a standardized format such as CycloneDX or SPDX that encodes version, license, and repository information.

- Feed the SBOM into a vulnerability scanner, either as a standalone operation in CI or coupled tightly via Bazel's custom rule extensions.

- Collect and analyze the vulnerability scan results; map findings to enforceable policies, for example, via severity thresholds or allowed exceptions.

- Integrate feedback loops into the Bazel build pipeline to either report or block builds on critical security vulnerabilities.

One effective practice is wrapping external dependency fetch operations within Bazel `repository_rules` to include additional validation phases. Customized repository rules can invoke license and vulnerability scanners during the external repository fetch, thereby ensuring that only compliant and secure dependencies are materialized into the build environment. This approach aligns dependency auditing with Bazel's philosophy of upfront correctness and deterministic inputs.

Programmatic extensions leveraging the Starlark language facilitate embedding policy logic directly inside Bazel builds. For instance, custom Starlark rules may parse external repository metadata and invoke external scanning tools, returning actionable results that influence the build's success or failure. While Bazel itself does not natively perform vulnerability detection or license validation, this extensibility allows integration of best-of-breed scanning solutions alongside Bazel's robust build orchestration.

The synergy between Bazel's precise dependency management and automated auditing tools also enables organizations to maintain compliance with stringent regulatory frameworks such as the European Union's Cybersecurity Act or the U.S. Executive Order on Improving the Nation's Cybersecurity. Automated workflows reduce manual intervention and human error, enabling faster and more reliable delivery of software that honors open source licenses and minimizes exposure to known vulnerabilities.

Dependency auditing and license compliance in Bazel-based systems revolve around continuous visibility, automated enforcement, and effective integration of specialized scanners into the build lifecycle. By leveraging Bazel's dependency graph interrogation capabilities and combining them with state-of-the-art SBOM generation, license scanning, and vulnerability detection tooling, organizations achieve a high level of software supply chain integrity-an imperative in today's complex and fast-evolving software ecosystems.

7.4. Build Artifact Verification and Attestation

Ensuring the integrity and authenticity of build artifacts is a critical component in securing the software supply chain. Build artifact verification and attestation provide mechanisms that cryptographically validate the outputs of a build process and generate metadata serving as proof of provenance and fidelity. These mechanisms are fundamental to establishing trust, enabling compliance with rigorous security policies, and facilitating robust audit trails.

The process begins with cryptographic verification, which relies on hash functions and digital signatures applied to build outputs. A cryptographic hash function produces a fixed-length digest uniquely representing the artifact content. This digest acts as the artifact's fingerprint; any alteration in the artifact leads to a different digest, signaling tampering. Common algorithms such as SHA-256 or SHA-3 are widely used due to their collision resistance and computational efficiency.

Verification tools, embedded in continuous integration/continuous deployment (CI/CD) pipelines or supply chain security platforms, calculate and compare these digest values to expected values stored in secure registries or provenance attestations. Establishing a root of trust for these expected values is paramount, often performed through hardware security modules (HSMs) or trusted platform modules (TPMs), ensuring that verification baselines themselves are immune to compromise.

Digital signatures augment hashing by incorporating asymmetric cryptography, thereby authenticating the origin of the artifact in addition to its integrity. Signing the artifact's hash with a private key assigns non-repudiable ownership and origin identification. Verification involves checking this signature with the corresponding public key, providing a secure means to confirm that artifacts have not been altered and were produced by authorized entities.

Generation of attestation metadata extends beyond simple hash values and signatures. Attestations capture contextual information describing the build environment, tooling versions, source code revision identifiers, and compliance parameters. Formal specifications such as the in-toto provenance framework or the Supply Chain Levels for Software Artifacts (SLSA) define standardized schemas to represent this metadata in machine-verifiable formats, typically serialized as JSON or protobuf.

For example, an attestation object may include the builder identity, cryptographic hashes of inputs and outputs, timestamps, and measurement of the environment's state. Secure signing of attestations by build servers or orchestrators certifies the veracity of this information. Downstream consumers, such as deployment systems, auditors, or regulators, can verify these attestations to enforce policy constraints or validate artifact authenticity prior to acceptance.

To produce tamper-evident artifacts, layered approaches are employed. Artifact immutability in storage is enforced through append-only registries or content-addressable storage systems, where artifact names correspond to their hash values, inherently binding the artifact's identity to its content. Immutable ledger technologies, including blockchain-based timestamping or transparency logs like those employed in the Binary Authorization for Borg (BAfB) or Rekor transparent logs, provide publicly verifiable records of artifacts and attestations, enhancing auditability and non-repudiation.

Integration of verification and attestation tools within automated build systems ensures consistent enforcement throughout the build lifecycle. For example, leveraging tools such as `cosign` enables automated signing and verification of container images and artifacts. The following command illustrates the signing of a container image artifact using `cosign`:

```
cosign sign --key cosign.key example.com/myimage:latest
```

Verification of the signature can be performed as follows:

```
cosign verify --key cosign.pub example.com/myimage:latest
```

Such tools can also generate attestation statements adhering to in-toto provenance standards, capturing comprehensive metadata corresponding to the build event.

The enforcement of artifact verification and attestation provides multiple security guarantees:

- **Integrity**: Ensures artifacts have not been altered during or after the build process.

- **Origin Verification**: Confirms that artifacts originate from trusted and authorized build environments.

- **Non-repudiation**: Prevents denial of authorship or origination via cryptographic signatures.

- **Traceability**: Establishes an audit trail linking artifacts back to source code, build tools, and configurations.

- **Compliance**: Enables enforcement of organizational or regulatory policies through verifiable evidence of artifact provenance and integrity.

Finally, the processes outlined here assume the underlying security of all components involved, from key management to the build infrastructure itself. Improper handling of cryptographic keys, inadequate build environment isolation, or lack of secure boot processes can undermine the guarantees provided by verification and attestation. Consequently, integrating hardware-based root of trust elements, implementing strict access controls, and continuously monitoring build environments are essential adjunct measures.

Build artifact verification and attestation form a cornerstone in securing modern software supply chains. Applying cryptographic hashing and signing techniques alongside comprehensive attestation metadata generation enables the production of tamper-evident artifacts. These mechanisms provide effective controls for compliance, auditability, and trustworthiness, which are indispensable in today's risk-conscious development ecosystems.

7.5. Managing and Rotating Secrets

Handling credentials and secrets securely within build pipelines is paramount to maintaining the integrity and confidentiality of software systems. In Bazel pipelines, where build reproducibility and hermeticity are emphasized, secrets such as API keys, private certificates, and access tokens must be managed with rigor to prevent inadvertent exposure and reduce attack surfaces.

One fundamental principle is to avoid embedding secrets directly in source code or configuration files that reside inside the repository. Instead, secrets should be injected dynamically at build or runtime stages, minimizing their footprint within the build graph and source control history. Bazel's sandboxing and remote execution capabilities enhance security by isolating build actions; however, these features must be carefully leveraged to ensure secrets are not leaked into caches, logs, or intermediate artifacts.

Externalizing Secrets Using Environment Variables and Secret Stores

A common approach is to externalize secrets and provide them to Bazel actions as environment variables or mounted files. For example, a CI system or a local developer environment can expose secrets through environment variables that Bazel rules consume at build time. This strategy enables secret injection without hard-coding and allows integration with centralized secret management systems such as HashiCorp Vault, AWS Secrets Manager, or GCP Secret Manager.

To minimize exposure:

- Environment variables containing secrets should be flagged with low verbosity logging to prevent accidental inclusion in build logs.

- Bazel remote caches must be configured to exclude any build outputs or metadata that contain sensitive information. This often requires segregating secret-dependent actions from cache hits or using cache key transformations.

- Secrets should be mounted as ephemeral files during sand-boxed build actions rather than persisted in workspace directories, leveraging Bazel's `runfiles` or sandbox input root features.

Using Bazel's `--action_env` and Starlark Rule APIs

Bazel provides the `--action_env` flag to propagate environment variables to build actions securely. This mechanism is preferable to baking values into rule attributes, as it prevents secrets from appearing in the action graph or build logs.

An example rule invocation to pass a secret environment variable:

```
bazel build //:my_target --action_env=API_TOKEN
```

In custom Starlark rules, environment variables can be accessed in `run_actions` without embedding secrets into the rule definition:

```
def _impl(ctx):
    ctx.actions.run(
        outputs=[ctx.outputs.executable],
```

```
    inputs=ctx.files.srcs,
    executable=ctx.executable.tool,
    env={"API_TOKEN": ctx.configuration.env.get("API_TOKEN")
  },
    arguments=["--do-something"],
)
```

This pattern isolates secrets to action execution contexts and avoids retention in build metadata.

Minimizing Secret Lifecycles and Scope

Following the principle of least privilege, secrets should have narrowly defined scopes and lifetimes. Short-lived tokens or ephemeral credentials reduce risk if compromised. Bazel pipelines should integrate automated secret rotation mechanisms synchronized with CI/CD workflows. For example:

- CI pipelines request short-duration tokens immediately before build stages.

- Secret-fetching steps encapsulate retrieval logic with proper authentication.

- Expiration triggers enforce forced build failures if secrets are outdated.

By automatically rotating secrets, leaked credentials become rapidly obsolete, constraining attacker opportunities.

Avoiding Secret Leakage Through Build Outputs and Logs

Secrets often leak unintentionally through logging and artifact generation. Bazel's deterministic build model helps mitigate this risk but requires discipline:

- Actions that consume secrets should never echo them to standard output or error streams.

- Logs generated by actions must be scanned or sanitized before archiving.

- Generated artifacts containing secrets, such as config files or certificates, should be handled as `private` or `runfiles` that do not propagate to downstream dependencies.

Tools like `bazel aquery` and `bazel cquery` can be used to analyze action graphs and detect any unintended secret propagation paths.

Pattern: Secret Injection via Repository Rules

Repository rules are specialized Starlark constructs that fetch external dependencies. They offer a controlled surface to inject secrets at fetch time without polluting the build graph. For instance, a `repository_rule` can use environment variables within its implementation function to authenticate against private artifact registries or secret endpoints:

```
def _private_repo_impl(ctx):
    token = ctx.os.environ.get("PRIVATE_REPO_TOKEN")
    if token is None:
        fail("PRIVATE_REPO_TOKEN not set")
    # Use token to authenticate and download dependency
    ...
    ctx.download(url, output)

private_repo = repository_rule(
    implementation=_private_repo_impl,
    attrs={"url": attr.string(mandatory=True)},
)
```

This confines secret usage to the repository fetching phase, avoiding exposure downstream.

Secure Secret Storage and Access Control

In build environments integrated with enterprise secret management solutions, Bazel pipelines interface with these services through highly privileged agents or tokens restricted by policy. Such integration requires:

- Strong authentication methods to access secret stores, e.g., mutual TLS, short-lived OAuth tokens.

- Fine-grained access control policies limiting which build targets or developers can retrieve secrets.

- Audit logging of all secret access requests to detect anomalous behavior.

These controls complement Bazel's sandbox by safeguarding secrets at the orchestration and infrastructure levels.

Combined Strategies for Robust Secret Management

Achieving effective secret management in Bazel pipelines involves combining multiple strategies:

- Externalize secrets away from source code and build graphs.

- Use environment variables or ephemeral file mounts during sandbox playback.

- Leverage short-lived tokens with automated rotation synchronized to pipeline execution.

- Employ repository rules for secret-dependent dependency fetching.

- Restrict logging and artifact generation that might contain sensitive information.

- Connect securely to enterprise secret management services enforcing access policies.

This layered defense reduces the attack surface and ensures that secrets remain transient, isolated, and protected throughout the entire Bazel build lifecycle.

In essence, managing and rotating secrets in Bazel pipelines demands a rigorous approach that balances usability with security.

Properly implemented, these practices protect critical credentials from exposure, supporting secure and reproducible software delivery at scale.

7.6. Integrating Static and Dynamic Analyses

Integrating static analyzers, linters, and dynamic security tools within Bazel's build framework requires a systematic approach that leverages Bazel's extensible rule system, sandboxed execution environment, and dependency graph awareness. This integration enables continuous security validation by embedding both early-stage code inspection and run-time behavior verification directly into the automated build pipeline. The combined utilization of these methodologies enhances vulnerability detection precisely at developer commit time and during integration testing.

Static analyzers and linters operate primarily by inspecting source code to identify potential security vulnerabilities, coding standard violations, and maintainability issues without executing the program. Bazel supports their incorporation by defining custom genrule or sh_binary targets wrapped inside repository_rule or toolchain configurations when appropriate. These targets encapsulate invocation scripts for analyzers such as clang-tidy, Bandit, or ESLint. Their outputs can be extracted and handled through the use of Bazel's test rules, enabling failure conditions when violations exist.

Consider the following emblematic example integrating a Python linter, pylint, as a Bazel test target for source files under the path //src:py_linter:

```
sh_test(
    name = "py_linter",
    srcs = ["pylint_wrapper.sh"],
    data = glob(["src/**/*.py"]),
    args = ["src/"],
    size = "small",
    timeout = "short",
```

```
)
```

The shell script `pylint_wrapper.sh` systematically runs pylint against all Python files and exits with an error code if issues surpass the configured threshold. By marking this target as a `sh_test`, Bazel's test execution phase integrates code quality validation seamlessly into the build graph. Should static analysis or linting fail, downstream targets depending on `py_linter` will be flagged as failed, effectively enforcing security gates early.

Dynamic security tools complement static approaches by analyzing the program behavior at runtime to uncover vulnerabilities related to memory safety, concurrency, and input validation that static analysis may miss. Tools such as AddressSanitizer, ThreadSanitizer, or runtime instrumentation frameworks (e.g., dynamic taint analysis) integrate through Bazel by building instrumented binaries and launching controlled test executions as dedicated `sh_test` or test rules.

For instance, embedding AddressSanitizer-enabled builds involves modifying the C++ compilation rule to inject the sanitizer flags and specifying a special test rule:

```
cc_binary(
    name = "instrumented_app",
    srcs = ["app.cc"],
    copts = ["-fsanitize=address", "-fno-omit-frame-pointer"],
    linkopts = ["-fsanitize=address"],
)

cc_test(
    name = "instrumented_app_test",
    srcs = ["app_test.cc"],
    deps = [":instrumented_app"],
    copts = ["-fsanitize=address", "-fno-omit-frame-pointer"],
    linkopts = ["-fsanitize=address"],
)
```

Running `bazel test //:instrumented_app_test` triggers the instrumented binary to execute under sanitizer supervision, detecting runtime memory violations which cause test failures if any are encountered. This integration elevates runtime security checks as an intrinsic part of continuous integration (CI).

Bridging static and dynamic analyses within Bazel is further enhanced by orchestrating these tools in defined execution phases linked within build targets and test suites. It is a recommended practice to separate purely static checks, which are typically fast and can be executed on every incremental build, from heavier dynamic tests that are appropriate for nightly builds or gated pipelines due to their runtime costs.

The continuous security integration model enforces several key patterns:

- Modularization of analyzers and tools as Bazel test targets, enabling fine-grained dependency control and parallel execution.

- Strict failure propagation by enforcing exit codes and utilizing `test` rule semantics for analyzer and dynamic tool invocations.

- Use of Bazel's `tag` mechanism and test size annotations to classify tests by runtime and resource consumption, controlling execution scheduling.

- Aggregation of results via Bazel's test summary XML output, suitable for consumption by CI dashboard tools for real-time security feedback.

An illustration of a combined pipeline target wiring multiple analyses could be structured as follows:

```
alias(
    name = "continuous_security_checks",
    actual = ":static_analysis_and_lint_tests",
)

test_suite(
    name = "static_analysis_and_lint_tests",
```

and developer workflows. This inventory must capture not only the static structural elements but also dynamic behavioral characteristics, such as build triggers, caching mechanisms, and incremental rebuild patterns. Quantitative metrics-build times, cache hit rates, test coverage, and failure modes-should be gathered to paint an empirical picture of current performance and pain points.

This empirical baseline enables the identification of core risk vectors inherent in the migration process. Risks typically manifest as environmental complexity, tightly coupled or undocumented dependencies, platform-specific behaviors, and resource allocation constraints. Each risk factor must be catalogued with an associated probability and impact estimate. For example, incomplete dependency graphs or reliance on non-hermetic tools elevate the probability of migration friction and extend validation cycles. Understanding these dimensions is critical for realistic timeline projection and resource scoping.

Constructing a phased migration plan necessitates decomposing the overall transition into manageable, incremental stages that progressively align legacy workflows with Bazel's architectural paradigms. The initial phase should prioritize pilot projects that feature representative, non-critical components exhibiting well-understood dependency structures. This conservative approach mitigates risk while building organizational confidence. Early successes can be leveraged to gather feedback, refine Bazel build configurations, and perfect integration scripts.

Subsequent phases expand breadth and depth, incorporating more complex targets, integrating platform-specific build steps, and embedding Bazel into continuous integration pipelines. At each phase, distinct milestones must be defined with clear deliverables, such as successful Bazel builds for a target subset, reduced build times, or improved cache utilization metrics. These milestones facilitate objective progress tracking and create natural review points for stakeholders.

Establishing explicit success criteria is paramount to evaluate whether each phase aligns with strategic goals. Common criteria encompass incrementally improved build stability, reproducibility, and performance consistent with or exceeding legacy systems. Additional factors include developer adoption rates, reduction in flaky builds, and measurable improvements in feedback cycles. Success criteria must be quantifiable and agreed upon prior to migration commencement to avoid ambiguity in progress assessment.

Stakeholder alignment represents a critical, ongoing component of migration planning. Effective communication channels should be instituted among developers, build engineers, product managers, and operations teams. Defining roles and responsibilities ensures that configuration ownership, troubleshooting processes, and decision-making authority are clear. Regular status reports, open forums for feedback, and transparent documentation foster a shared understanding of challenges and successes. This inclusivity mitigates resistance and engenders a culture of collective ownership.

Technical risk assessment should incorporate a comprehensive dependency analysis. Automated tools capable of extracting and visualizing dependency graphs enable the detection of implicit dependencies and circular references that impede Bazel adoption. Addressing these issues early through modularization or refactoring reduces the system's surface area for migration disruptions.

Another critical risk dimension involves the integration of external, non-Bazel-compatible tools or proprietary build steps. Strategies to mitigate these issues involve encapsulation through custom Bazel rules or gradual replacement with Bazel-native equivalents. Allocating dedicated time and expertise for rule development in the migration plan prevents downstream bottlenecks.

Phased rollout also implies iterative validation through continuous integration systems. Early phases must incorporate rigorous automated tests that verify both build correctness and performance metrics. It is advisable to parallelize Bazel builds alongside legacy systems initially, allowing incremental replacements rather than a big-bang switch. This approach facilitates immediate rollback if critical issues arise and provides confidence in the Bazel-based build artifacts.

The migration plan should explicitly incorporate contingency measures for unexpected delays or failures. Buffer periods, fallback plans, and escalation paths must be detailed, ensuring project resiliency. Additionally, budgetary considerations should reflect the inclusion of training, tooling adaptation, and possible third-party consulting to address expertise gaps.

Assessment and migration planning for Bazel adoption require a methodical, data-driven approach that balances technical rigor with organizational readiness. Comprehensive environment evaluation, risk identification, and the construction of phased milestones underpin a controlled transition. By defining clear success criteria and aligning stakeholders through transparent communication, organizations can navigate inherent complexities and realize the benefits of robust, scalable Bazel build infrastructures.

8.2. Automated Refactoring and Tooling

The scale and complexity inherent in modern software ecosystems necessitate a robust, automated approach to codebase and build system migration. Manual refactoring of large code repositories is prohibitively time-consuming and error-prone, making automated tooling essential for reliable and efficient transitions. Automated refactoring and tooling encompass scripts, migration frameworks, and integrated development environment (IDE) plugins designed to systematically convert code constructs and build definitions while minimizing developer disruption.

Automated tooling begins with the identification and formalization of transformation rules that capture the syntactic and semantic changes required during migration. These rules are typically encoded as pattern matches that locate deprecated or legacy constructs, paired with corresponding templates for their modern equivalents. For example, in transitioning from an older build system to a new one, specific build rules or macros can be programmatically replaced using abstract syntax tree (AST) manipulation or domain-specific language (DSL) parsers that understand the build language. This method ensures code transformations are consistent and maintainable.

Several categories of tools support automated refactoring:

- **Source-to-source transformers**: These tools parse source code into an intermediate representation (such as an AST), apply transformation rules, and regenerate code in the target format. They effectively enable syntax-aware rewrites while preserving semantics.

- **Build rule converters**: Specialized parsers and generators for build configurations parse existing rule files, map deprecated constructs into contemporary equivalents, and generate new build descriptions that integrate seamlessly with updated tooling.

- **Migration frameworks**: Higher-level orchestrations that coordinate multiple transformation steps, offer rollback capabilities, and provide reporting on migration progress and issues.

Automation scripts often integrate tightly with version control systems (VCS) to enable incremental migration strategies. By breaking down the monolithic migration into smaller, manageable chunks, developers can reduce risk and isolate errors efficiently. Commonly, a branch-based workflow is adopted whereby changes

Ultimately, the goal of automated refactoring and tooling is to reduce the cognitive and operational overhead placed on development teams during large-scale transitions. By combining precise transformation capabilities, continuous validation, and seamless developer experience, such tooling significantly accelerates the pace of modernization while preserving system stability.

```
WORKFLOW EXCERPT FROM AUTOMATED MIGRATION PIPELINE:

1. Scan repository to create a model of existing build rules and code depende
nc ies.
2. Generate transformation maps encoding legacy-to-new constructs.
3. Apply source-to-source transformations iteratively across modules.
4. Run incremental builds and diagnostics on migrated subsets.
5. Collect test results and static analysis reports.
6. Flag and isolate failures for manual developer intervention.
7. Merge validated changes gradually into target branch.
8. Update documentation and developer guides accordingly.
```

8.3. Incremental Adoption Strategies

Incremental adoption of Bazel within existing development workflows demands carefully designed strategies that prioritize coexistence with legacy build systems, controlled onboarding of teams and components, and rigorous validation throughout the migration phases. Organizations typically cannot replace their entire build infrastructure in a single effort without incurring substantial disruption. Hence, a gradual, experiment-driven approach that leverages hybrid builds, selective migration gates, and iterative integration patterns offers a practical pathway toward effective Bazel adoption.

A fundamental principle in incremental adoption is maintaining operability of legacy build systems alongside Bazel. This coexistence ensures business continuity and provides a safety net during migration. To achieve this, Bazel can be introduced as an alternative build system for isolated subsystems, libraries, or specific targets without reorganizing the complete repository or build graph.

Teams can start by defining Bazel BUILD files only for a subset of modules, while the remainder of the system continues to use the original build tools.

Introducing wrappers and abstractions that unify build invocation across systems is essential to avoid fragmentation. A common approach is to implement meta-build scripts or tooling layers that detect the context and invoke Bazel or legacy builds as appropriate. This allows developers to initiate builds uniformly and access artifacts seamlessly, regardless of the underlying build backend. Additionally, build artifact compatibility and cache consistency must be carefully managed, possibly via artifact translation steps or shared dependency repositories.

Hybrid builds refer to the execution of Bazel alongside legacy build systems within the same CI/CD pipeline or local build environment. By segmenting the codebase into Bazel-native and legacy-managed partitions, hybrid strategies enable teams to onboard gradually. A practical practice is to start with low-risk, independently testable components-libraries, utilities, or service boundaries-that do not tightly couple with large parts of the system.

To facilitate this, Bazel's flexible workspace and repository rules allow inclusion of external, non-Bazel-managed dependencies. For instance, external repositories can encapsulate legacy-built binaries or artifacts, enabling Bazel targets to depend upon them without requiring full migration upfront. This approach preserves the internal dependency graph integrity within Bazel-managed components, while still leveraging legacy build outputs as inputs.

Iterative onboarding encourages frequent but small scope Bazel migration increments, reducing risk and easing validation. The strategy can employ feature flags or build profile switches to toggle between Bazel and legacy builds on a per-target basis, granting granular control over the migration progression. Developer training and documentation should accompany onboarding to mitigate adoption resistance and establish internal expertise incrementally.

Incremental Bazel adoption intersects closely with continuous integration and quality assurance practices. Introducing migration gates-automated build and test checkpoints-ensures every migration step preserves correctness and performance characteristics. These gates validate both Bazel-managed and legacy builds, comparing outputs, runtime behaviors, and performance metrics to detect regressions early.

Migration gates may include:

- **Build output equivalence checks**: Verifying that Bazel builds produce functionally identical binaries, libraries, or artifacts compared to legacy builds.

- **Cross-system integration tests**: Exercising components built via Bazel with legacy-built components and vice versa to validate compatibility.

- **Performance benchmarks**: Ensuring that incremental Bazel builds do not degrade build speed or developer productivity relative to legacy workflows.

- **Static analysis and lint enforcement**: Running Bazel's built-in analysis to catch dependency or configuration issues early.

Automated gating mechanisms help build team confidence in the adoption process and act as fail-safe measures to avoid propagating errors downstream. Migration gates can be integrated into CI pipelines with conditional execution, dynamically adjusting to the current scope of Bazel adoption.

An effective incremental adoption pattern involves iteratively extending Bazel's coverage rather than a big-bang migration. Typical patterns include:

- **Library-by-Library Migration**: Incrementally converting individual libraries or modules to Bazel BUILD files while maintaining compatibility through dependency shims and wrapper targets.

- **Test-Driven Migration**: Prioritizing test code migration first to leverage Bazel's robust test execution and caching capabilities. This enables rapid feedback cycles and accelerates adoption momentum.

- **Feature Toggle Integration**: Using feature toggles or environment variables to dynamically switch between Bazel and legacy builds per component or target to isolate impacts.

- **Repository Segmentation**: For monolithic repositories, introducing Bazel progressively by partitioning repository sections as sub-workspaces or external repositories, enabling independent Bazel adoption cycles.

- **Dependency Graph Refinement**: Gradually rebuilding and optimizing the dependency graph within Bazel, identifying unnecessary dependencies or cycles that may have been obscured in legacy build descriptors.

Each pattern emphasizes rapid feedback, modular migration boundaries, and rollback potential. They facilitate evolutionary rather than revolutionary change, minimizing the burden on developers and infrastructure.

Consider a codebase where a set of core libraries is still built using make, while application binaries are to be migrated incrementally to Bazel. One approach is to create Bazel BUILD targets that declare external make-built binaries as filegroups or genrule outputs. Concurrently, Bazel-managed application targets depend on these externally defined artifacts.

```
libcore.a:
    gcc -c core.c -o core.o
    ar rcs libcore.a core.o
```

Such patterns allow gradual migration with clear deprecation warnings. The compatibility matrix for supported versions should be continuously updated and validated via automated tests. A dedicated test suite should capture behavioral contracts and flag regressions during refactors or Bazel version upgrades.

Isolating Stable Interfaces

Separation of stable public interfaces from internal implementation details enhances maintainability. Define a small set of well-documented entry points as the "public API" of the rule or macro with explicit input and output objects or attributes. Internal implementation functions, helper macros, or complex logic should remain hidden within private .bzl files or nested functions that are not intended for external invocation.

This encapsulation reduces the risk of accidental misuse and increases the freedom to refactor internals without widespread disruptions. It also facilitates incremental improvements by replacing internal modules independently, provided the public interface contracts remain unchanged.

Use of Abstraction Layers

Where multiple rules share similar patterns, computation logic, or resource handling, introduce explicit abstraction layers to reduce code duplication. Common abstractions manifest as utility functions, shared rule templates, or higher-order macros that assemble rules from simpler components.

Example: a parameterized factory macro that generates rules with variant configurations:

```
def rule_factory(name, srcs, lang="cc", extra_attrs = {}):
    if lang == "cc":
        return cc_binary(name = name, srcs = srcs, **extra_attrs)
    elif lang == "py":
        return py_binary(name = name, srcs = srcs, **extra_attrs)
    else:
        fail("Unsupported language: " + lang)
```

These abstractions improve maintainability by localizing changes and enable easier onboarding of new developers who learn idiomatic patterns rather than isolated procedural code. However, abstraction should not be pursued indiscriminately; complexity must be balanced against clarity.

Proactive Maintenance and Automation

Proactive maintenance anticipates future changes and strives to detect compatibility issues early. Incorporate the following automation and process-driven practices:

- **Continuous Integration Testing:** Automated builds and tests that run for every change minimize regressions. Include tests that cover common and edge-case rule usage patterns, ensuring that rule semantics remain consistent.

- **Linting and Style Enforcement:** Custom Starlark linters or use of generic syntax checkers help maintain code quality and readability.

- **Deprecation Warnings:** Programmatically emit warnings in rule implementation paths for deprecated attributes or usages, guiding users to upgrade.

- **Documentation and Examples:** Maintain up-to-date, comprehensive documentation with usage examples, explicitly noting stable APIs and supported versions.

Managing External Dependencies

Custom rules and extensions often rely on external toolchains, repositories, or even code-generation utilities. To minimize maintenance burden stemming from external changes:

- Use explicit version pins for external dependencies in WORKSPACE files. Avoid floating versions that may introduce untested breaking changes.

- Encapsulate dependency access through macros that can evolve independently of the rules consuming them.

- Maintain a clear upgrade procedure, including validation steps verifying that upstream changes do not disrupt builds.

Refactoring and Modularization

As complexity grows, regular refactoring of Starlark code is essential to avoid technical debt accumulation. Break large monolithic .bzl files into smaller, logically organized modules grouped by functionality or domain. For example, separate rule definitions, utility functions, and third-party wrappers into distinct files:

- `rules/build_rules.bzl`

- `utils/helpers.bzl`

- `third_party/protobuf_defs.bzl`

This modularity improves discoverability and parallelizes development efforts. It also permits fine-grained code ownership and targeted review practices.

Handling Evolving Bazel Platform Features

Bazel's own platform and APIs-such as aspects, toolchains, configuration transitions, and Starlark language enhancements-frequently evolve. To minimize breakage from Bazel upgrades:

- Regularly monitor Bazel release notes and migrate to new recommended idioms proactively.

- Encapsulate usage of advanced platform features behind stable abstraction layers.

- Limit dependencies on deprecated or experimental APIs.

- Incorporate Bazel version gating in build scripts to selectively enable features.

Sustainable maintenance of custom Starlark rules and extensions depends on a combination of forward-thinking design, rigorous version control, modular abstraction, and automated verification. Maintaining stable interfaces while fostering extensibility and improving developer ergonomics ensures that build logic evolves gracefully alongside the projects it supports, maintaining high reliability and performance over time.

8.5. Upgrades, Compatibility, and Deprecations

Managing Bazel upgrades, adapting to rule deprecations, and responding to upstream changes require a combination of tactical rigor and strategic foresight. The complexity of Bazel's evolving ecosystem demands robust dependency mapping, comprehensive automated testing, and streamlined communication workflows to ensure minimal disruption and sustainable system evolution.

A foundational practice is to maintain an explicit and continuously updated dependency graph for all workspace components. This map should delineate internal targets, external repositories, toolchains, and custom rules, capturing both direct and transitive relationships. Tools such as `bazel query` enable extraction of these dependencies programmatically. For example, the following command reveals direct dependencies of a target:

```
bazel query 'deps(//myapp:app)' --output graph > deps.dot
```

Visualizing the dependency graph regularly aids in pinpointing which components will be affected upon upgrading Bazel or modifying rules. Integrating this into CI pipelines ensures that stakeholders have real-time visibility of the impact scope before initiating changes.

211

Automated testing frameworks must be configured to cover not only functional correctness but also build integrity across version boundaries. This entails test suites that run against the current stable Bazel release alongside upcoming versions identified via nightly or release-candidate channels. Test matrices can be orchestrated with buildkite, Jenkins, or GitHub Actions using a parameterized setup:

```
jobs:
  build_and_test:
    strategy:
      matrix:
        bazel_version: [4.2.1, 5.0.0-rc1, latest]
    steps:
      - run: |
          bazel --bazelrc=.bazelrc-$bazel_version build //...
          bazel --bazelrc=.bazelrc-$bazel_version test //...
```

Such concurrent validation detects regressions or deprecated API usage before widespread impact, enabling timely remediation.

Rule deprecations present a nuanced challenge. The first step involves monitoring Bazel's release notes, GitHub issue tracker, and relevant mailing lists or chat channels for formal deprecation announcements and migration guides. Annotating custom rules with explicit `deprecation` and `replacement` metadata can automate discovery of deprecated targets within the workspace. For instance:

```
def _old_rule_impl(ctx):
    ctx.warn("old_rule is deprecated since Bazel 5.0; use
    new_rule instead")

old_rule = rule(
    implementation = _old_rule_impl,
    attrs = {...},
    deprecation = True,
    replacement = "//rules:new_rule",
)
```

Refactoring efforts should prioritize replacing deprecated rules incrementally, starting with low-risk components to establish confidence. Employing macros and aspect-oriented programming reduces repetitive migrations and centralizes compatibility logic, facilitating rollbacks if necessary.

Upstream changes frequently cascade downstream in unforeseen ways. Establishing a defined communication workflow is critical to manage this risk effectively. Ideally, a designated Bazel stewardship team or maintainer group assumes responsibility for tracking upstream progress, triaging issues, and synthesizing change advisories. A recommended workflow includes:

- **Regular monitoring:** Subscribe to Bazel release announcements, follow RFCs and proposals, and review pull requests in the main Bazel repository.

- **Impact assessment:** Leverage the dependency graph to identify components impacted by changes.

- **Regression testing:** Trigger build and test jobs automatically upon detection of upstream release candidates.

- **Internal communications:** Circulate upgrade plans and known issues via mailing lists, dashboards, or team meetings.

- **Feedback loop:** Report issues encountered during upgrades back to Bazel's issue tracker with detailed reproduction steps and logs.

Integrating these workflows with version control mechanisms such as continuous integration branches specifically for Bazel upgrades allows safe experimentation without destabilizing mainline development.

A practical pattern is to introduce automated tooling that generates upgrade reports summarizing altered dependencies, deprecated rule usage, and test outcomes. A script fragment implementing this report may utilize bazel query combined with git diffs:

```
# List targets using deprecated rules
bazel query 'kind(rule, //...:*)' --output label_kind | \
  grep deprecated_rule_name > deprecated_targets.txt

# Generate list of changed files between versions
git diff --name-only bazel-4.2.1 bazel-5.0.0 > changed_files.txt

# Compose summary
echo "Deprecated targets:" > upgrade_report.txt
cat deprecated_targets.txt >> upgrade_report.txt
echo "\nChanged files:" >> upgrade_report.txt
cat changed_files.txt >> upgrade_report.txt
```

Embedding upgrade report generation into CI ensures proactive risk management and transparent decision-making.

In sum, the interplay between Bazel's upgrade cadence, rule lifecycle, and upstream evolution demands a holistic approach. Comprehensive dependency mapping, exhaustive versioned testing, active deprecation management, and disciplined communications converge to reduce upgrade friction. These practices empower engineering organizations to harness Bazel's advancements while sustaining robust, predictable build environments.

8.6. Metrics and Health Monitoring

Continuous monitoring of the Bazel build system is critical for maintaining high performance, ensuring reliability, and preserving codebase quality. Proactive detection of regressions in build speed, system infrastructure, and code correctness allows teams to respond swiftly and mitigate the impact on development velocity. Establishing an effective monitoring framework involves comprehensive instrumentation, intuitive visualization through dashboards, and a robust alerting mechanism tailored for build-specific metrics.

Instrumentation begins with integrating metric collectors at strategic points within the Bazel execution and the supporting infras-

214

tructure. Key metrics to capture include build latency, cache hit rates, test failure rates, and resource utilization of build machines. Bazel's built-in profiling tools can output trace files providing fine-grained insights into the execution graph and critical path analysis. These profiles serve as invaluable resources to identify bottlenecks such as long-running actions or excessive dependency loading.

Beyond Bazel itself, instrumentation should extend into the continuous integration (CI) environment, capturing build queue times, worker availability, and artifact storage latencies. Exporting these metrics in a standardized format, such as Prometheus exposition format, enables seamless aggregation and retention over time. Instrumentation libraries, designed for minimal overhead, ensure there is no noticeable degradation of build performance due to monitoring.

Once collected, metrics need to be aggregated and visualized in dashboards that reveal both an instantaneous snapshot and historical trends. Configurable dashboards display key performance indicators (KPIs) such as:

- Average and percentile-based build durations over time.

- Cache hit/miss ratios, segmented by remote and local caches.

- Test execution times and pass/fail rates with breakdowns by test suites.

- CPU, memory, and network usage across build executors.

- Counts and classifications of build errors or warnings.

Aggregation at different temporal resolutions facilitates the correlation of performance anomalies with specific code commits or infrastructural changes. Custom dashboard panels can embed dependency graph snapshots or Bazel query outputs to contextualize regressions.

An effective alerting system is vital for early identification of abnormalities. Defining thresholds and anomaly detection rules tailored to build health metrics enables automated notifications to development and infrastructure teams. Alerts can be based on static thresholds (e.g., build time exceeding 95th percentile) or dynamic baselines derived from historical data (e.g., sudden drop in cache hit rate). Alerting channels typically include emails, chatops integrations, and incident management systems.

To illustrate, consider the following Prometheus alert rule for detecting an unexpected increase in build duration:

```
alert: BazelBuildDurationRegression
expr: avg_over_time(bazel_build_duration_seconds[1h]) > 1.5 *
    avg_over_time(bazel_build_duration_seconds[7d])
for: 10m
labels:
  severity: warning
annotations:
  summary: "Build duration regression detected"
  description: "The average build duration over the last hour is
    50% higher than the previous week's average."
```

Triggers such as this enable teams to react before regressions compound and impact broader workflows. Integrating these alerts with on-call rotations ensures fast triage of potential issues.

Beyond automated alerting, historical metric retention supports capacity planning and optimization decisions. Analyzing long-term trends can reveal detrimental growth in build times due to codebase complexity, enabling teams to prioritize technical debt remediation or rework of build rules. Health monitoring data also underpins predictive models for build resource scaling, leading to more efficient CI platforms.

Codebase quality indirectly influences build health, and metrics related to test coverage, static analysis violations, and code churn should be incorporated in the monitoring framework. Correlating these quality metrics with build times and failures aids in pinpointing problematic areas of the repository needing focused attention.

Additionally, monitoring test flakiness rates offers insight into reliability, directly affecting developer confidence and iteration speed.

Instrumentation should be implemented with extensibility and security in mind. Collectors must avoid sensitive data leakage and comply with organizational privacy policies. Moreover, the monitoring system should gracefully handle failures and ensure metric collection does not interfere with build correctness or developer productivity.

A comprehensive approach to metrics and health monitoring for Bazel builds integrates detailed instrumentation, informative dashboards, and precise alerting. These components form a feedback loop that improves build performance, guards infrastructure reliability, and maintains code quality by enabling early detection and rapid resolution of regressions.

Chapter 9

Future Directions and Open Challenges

Bazel is constantly evolving, and the future of build engineering is being rewritten with every contribution. This chapter surveys the horizon—spotlighting experimental innovations, looming technical challenges, and the transformative opportunities that lie ahead. Whether you want to shape Bazel's direction or simply keep your builds future-proof, these insights prepare you to lead where build systems are headed next.

9.1. Recent and Upcoming Innovations in Bazel

Bazel, having matured into a robust and extensible build system, continues to evolve with features designed to optimize build efficiency, enhance developer experience, and scale across complex monorepos and diverse platforms. The recent and forthcoming innovations reflect a distinct emphasis on incremental performance, improved tooling, and deeper integration with emerging technologies, which collectively benefit developers, teams, and the broader software build ecosystem.

One of the notable recent additions to Bazel is the introduction of *Bazel's remote execution API enhancements*. These improvements enable more fine-grained control over caching and execution strategies, reducing redundant computations and network overhead in distributed build environments. With enhanced remote caching, incremental builds can now detect changes more precisely, avoiding unnecessary recompilation and accelerating feedback loops. For teams operating at scale with large codebases, this translates to substantial reductions in build times and an increase in overall productivity.

Closely related is the expansion of Bazel's *remote execution platform support*. The system now allows seamless integration with cloud providers' managed execution services, such as Google Cloud Build and AWS CodeBuild, enabling organizations to offload resource-intensive tasks transparently. The innovation here lies in Bazel's ability to dynamically select execution platforms based on workload characteristics and environment constraints, which encourages cost-effective use of infrastructure without sacrificing build speed.

The *Starlark language*, Bazel's domain-specific language for build rule definition, has also undergone meaningful advancements. The Bazel team has introduced experimental features such as first-class support for asynchronous computations and improved APIs for manipulating complex data structures. These enhancements empower rule authors to write more expressive and efficient build logic, fostering customization without compromising Bazel's deterministic build guarantees. The evolving Starlark ecosystem pushes the limits of Bazel's extensibility, enabling adoption in increasingly diverse development contexts.

A major innovation with far-reaching impact is the upgrade of Bazel's *dependency management and module system*. The recently stabilized `modules` feature allows Bazel to more effectively manage external dependencies with strict versioning and conflict resolution. This system mirrors many capabilities long familiar from package managers in the broader software world but tailored to Bazel's unique build graph semantics. Multi-language repositories particularly benefit through consistent and hermetic dependency handling, improving reproducibility and simplifying maintenance overhead.

Furthermore, Bazel's *remote caching protocols* have adopted new hashing algorithms and metadata formats to optimize cache lookup times and reduce storage consumption. This technical refinement enables higher cache hit rates with lower latency across distributed environments, especially crucial in CI/CD pipeline integrations. Consequently, teams experience more efficient sharing of build artifacts between developers and build servers, fostering faster iteration cycles.

Among cultural and process-oriented innovations, Bazel's development community has prioritized enhanced *developer ergonomics*, reflected in improvements to tooling and diagnostics. The Bazel query language has been extended with more expressive operators and optimized execution plans, empowering engineers to gain deeper insights into build dependency graphs and swiftly identify bottlenecks. Coupled with new features in Bazel's integrated build event protocol, these changes facilitate richer real-time observability and debugging capabilities, supporting smoother onboarding and reducing cognitive load during complex troubleshooting.

Looking ahead, an area of keen interest within the Bazel ecosystem is the anticipated incorporation of *incremental compilation techniques adapted to modern programming languages*, such as Rust and Swift. These advances build upon Bazel's core incremental build mechanisms, aiming to dramatically reduce build times by precisely tracking minimal rebuild units within the compiler pipeline itself. Partial experimental work centered around compiler plugin architectures and fine-grained metadata generation already shows promising results, signaling a substantial leap forward in build efficiency for performance-critical projects.

Another imminent innovation includes improved *multi-platform support* targeting heterogeneous computing environments. Bazel is evolving to seamlessly handle cross-compilation scenarios, containerized development workflows, and integration with emerging hardware accelerators like GPUs and TPUs. The introduction of enhanced platform constraint handling mechanisms and toolchain abstractions enables Bazel to orchestrate reproducible builds across disparate execution contexts, thereby broadening its applicability in domains such as machine learning, embedded systems, and mobile development.

Collectively, these innovations embody Bazel's strategic trajectory toward being a versatile, scalable, and developer-friendly build platform tailored for modern software engineering challenges. For individual developers, these features yield faster feedback and more manageable build configurations. Teams benefit through improved consistency, reduced infrastructure costs, and superior collaboration workflows. At the ecosystem level, Bazel's evolving capabilities stimulate growth by facilitating integration with emerging technologies and promoting best practices in reproducible and efficient build processes.

As Bazel continues to push the boundaries of build automation, the interplay between incremental performance enhancements, language and platform support, and developer tooling will remain central to its ongoing evolution. This complex balance ensures Bazel not only meets the immediate needs of contemporary development but also anticipates future demands in increasingly heterogeneous and distributed build environments.

9.2. Bazel in Cloud-native and Serverless Environments

The adoption of Bazel within cloud-native and serverless platforms introduces both opportunities and complexities shaped by the paradigms of ephemeral compute, distributed orchestration, and highly dynamic scaling. Kubernetes, serverless frameworks, and related infrastructure provide distinct operational contexts that necessitate tailored Bazel integration strategies to harness its full potential in build, test, and deployment automation.

Integration Patterns for Kubernetes and Serverless Platforms

In Kubernetes environments, Bazel operates within containerized build workers orchestrated by the cluster scheduler. The typical integration pattern involves encapsulating Bazel in lightweight containers, which can be dynamically spawned on demand. This allows builds to leverage Kubernetes' inherent elasticity but introduces dependency on cluster resource scheduling and network latencies. Continuous integration (CI) pipelines frequently implement custom Kubernetes jobs that run Bazel builds within ephemeral pods, configured with resource requests and limits optimized to balance build speed and cluster utilization.

For serverless platforms such as AWS Lambda, Google Cloud Functions, or Azure Functions, the invocation model is event-driven and stateless, with strict execution time constraints. Here, Bazel's role often shifts from runtime compilation towards build artifact preprocessing executed outside the function's lifecycle. Integration often involves prebuilding fully packaged, minimal deployment units via Bazel and uploading these artifacts to object storage or specialized registries. Serverless deployment frameworks consume these prebuilt packages, vastly shrinking cold start times and minimizing function size, which are critical for cost control and performance.

Challenges Unique to Cloud-native Builds

Key challenges arise from the distributed, ephemeral nature of cloud builds. Unlike a monolithic on-premises build environment, cloud-native Bazel usage must contend with:

- **State Management:** Bazel's build cache and dependency graphs rely on persistent state. In Kubernetes or serverless contexts, ephemeral build containers or pods often lack persistent storage, mandating integration with external, network-accessible caches such as Remote Cache implementations (e.g., Google Cloud Storage, Amazon S3) using the Remote Execution API. Latency and cache eviction policies in these systems significantly impact build reproducibility and performance.

- **Scaling Build Workers:** Autoscaling of build executors to accommodate fluctuating workloads is feasible but complex. Over-provisioning clusters leads to resource waste, while conservative scaling delays build completion. Coordinating the lifecycle of Bazel workers with cluster autoscalers and managing work queues efficiently require custom resource management controllers or platform-native job queues integrated with Bazel's distributed execution mechanisms.

- **Network and Security Constraints:** Cloud-native environments are often subject to stringent network policies and multi-tenancy isolation. Bazel remote execution and caching necessitate secure, performant network channels. This drives the adoption of encrypted REST/GRPC communication and fine-grained access controls. Auditing build actions and ensuring provenance integrity become fundamental for compliance.

Scaling Strategies and Ephemeral Builds

Scaling Bazel builds in cloud environments involves balancing horizontal parallelism with infrastructure overhead. Kubernetes provides native job parallelism, but careful tuning is required to optimally split Bazel build "actions" across pods without incurring excessive coordination costs. Bazel's Remote Execution API facilitates offloading granular compilation and testing actions to remote workers, distributing jobs transparently.

Ephemeral builds within short-lived containers emphasize minimal startup times. Container images hosting Bazel must be stripped to essential components, and dependency fetching must be optimized through aggressive layering and cache sharing via Init Containers or sidecar proxies for artifact downloads. Build graphs are often partitioned to enable partial rebuilds, accelerating iterative development in ephemeral contexts.

The Remote Build Execution (RBE) paradigm gains importance, where a pool of persistent, shared workers perform Bazel actions on behalf of ephemeral invocations. This decouples the durability of the build environment from the ephemeral client, with results streamed back efficiently. Underlying systems must ensure consistency and fault tolerance to prevent incomplete or inconsistent builds.

Infrastructure Considerations

Effectively leveraging Bazel in cloud-native environments mandates rethinking underlying infrastructure:

- **Persistent Remote Caches:** Solutions such as Google Cloud Storage, Amazon S3, or dedicated cache servers provide backing to Bazel's Remote Cache. Configurations must minimize cache misses and stale artifacts. TTL policies and cache pruning strategies should align with project velocity and storage costs.

- **Build Farm Deployment:** When deploying remote execution servers, orchestrators like Kubernetes can host scalable build farms comprising worker pools, scheduler services, and cache proxies. Infrastructure-as-Code (IaC) templates provision and maintain these farms, allowing dynamic scaling, monitoring, and lifecycle management.

- **Security and Access Control:** Integration with cloud IAM enables role-based access control for build artifacts, logs, and compute resources. Secrets management for credentials used in remote execution or caching must be embedded securely within build containers or pods without introducing attack surfaces.

- **Telemetry and Debugging:** Cloud-native builds generate distributed traces spanning containers, storage, and network layers. Integrating Bazel's event logs with cloud monitoring and distributed tracing systems helps detect bottlenecks and failures, improving build reliability and developer productivity.

Bazel's platform-agnostic architecture combined with its remote execution and caching capabilities makes it well-suited for cloud-native adoption. Nonetheless, effective usage demands careful integration with ephemeral compute models, scalable infrastructure orchestration, and robust caching mechanisms. The shift to containerization and serverless invokes new operational trade-offs around build speed, state persistence, and security that must be addressed through tailored configuration and advanced infrastructure patterns. As cloud platforms continue evolving, Bazel serves as a foundational technology enabling reproducible, scalable, and efficient builds adapted to the mutable nature of modern distributed development environments.

9.3. Integrating AI/ML in Build and Test Optimization

Machine learning (ML) methodologies have emerged as pivotal enablers in optimizing software build and test processes, particularly in large-scale and continuous integration (CI) environments. The principal challenge addressed by these approaches is the efficient allocation of computational and temporal resources to accelerate feedback cycles without compromising quality assurance. This section examines contemporary research and early adoption exemplars that illustrate the use of predictive ML models targeting two primary optimization objectives: automatic split point identification in builds and test prioritization within testing pipelines.

Automatic split point identification involves segmenting monolithic build pipelines into smaller, manageable units that can be concurrently executed or selectively triggered. Traditionally, build splitting required manual heuristics or coarse-grained dependency analysis, often resulting in suboptimal pipeline configurations. Data-driven ML models now enable dynamic and fine-grained partitioning by learning from historical build metadata, code change patterns, runtime metrics, and dependency graphs. For example, supervised learning classifiers and clustering algorithms have been trained to predict optimal split points that minimize overall build latency while maintaining dependency correctness. Features leveraged typically include file modification frequencies, module interdependencies, resource consumption, and prior build durations.

One prominent approach employs reinforcement learning (RL) to adaptively refine split strategies based on cumulative pipeline performance feedback. Here, the RL agent models the build execution environment, iteratively exploring different segmentation schemes and receiving reward signals pertinent to build speed and test coverage quality. This continuous learning loop enables the system to respond to evolving codebases and changing infrastructure conditions. A case study from a large open-source project demonstrated that an RL-based splitter reduced average build time by approximately 25%, compared to static splitting heuristics.

Regarding test execution optimization, test prioritization seeks to reorder test cases to maximize early fault detection or minimize execution time within constrained testing budgets. The integration of ML facilitates predictive modeling of test outcomes and execution durations by exploiting features extracted from test history, code changes, coverage data, and runtime logs. Classification algorithms such as gradient-boosted trees and neural networks have been applied to estimate the likelihood of test failures given recent source changes, enabling risk-based prioritization that focuses on tests most relevant to current modifications.

An illustrative example includes the use of neural embeddings generated from code diffs, combined with historical test feedback, to rank tests dynamically. This approach enhances regression fault detection rates by emphasizing tests that previously identified defects in similar code regions. Additionally, unsupervised techniques, such as anomaly detection on test runtime patterns, have been employed to flag flaky or unstable tests, thus informing scheduling decisions that improve overall pipeline reliability.

Hybrid strategies also merge build and test optimization by jointly modeling the interdependencies between build segments and corresponding test sets. Multi-task learning architectures have been explored to concurrently predict optimal split points and test prioritization rankings, exploiting shared features to enhance model generalization. Such integrated frameworks facilitate coordinated scheduling decisions that further compress continuous delivery cycles.

Empirical evaluations from early adopters affirm the practical benefits of integrating AI/ML into build and test processes. For instance, a multinational technology company reported a 30% cumulative reduction in build and test throughput time by deploying

228

ML-driven split point identification coupled with test prioritization. Moreover, the system enabled adaptive pipeline reconfiguration in response to fluctuating resource availability and varying code change velocity, demonstrating robustness and scalability in production settings.

Challenges remain in achieving widespread deployment, notably the demand for large volumes of high-quality labeled data, model interpretability requirements, and integration complexity with existing DevOps toolchains. Research continues to address these issues by developing semi-supervised and transfer learning methods to lessen data dependency, explainable ML models to enhance user trust, and modular APIs for seamless toolchain integration.

The application of AI/ML techniques to predictive optimization of build and test execution represents a transformative advancement in continuous integration infrastructure. By leveraging historical operational data and sophisticated modeling, these methods provide automated, adaptive mechanisms for resource-efficient pipeline management. Current research trajectories and early industrial implementations point toward increasingly intelligent and resilient DevOps ecosystems that are central to meeting the demands of rapid and reliable software delivery.

9.4. Open Problems in Build Engineering

Despite decades of research and practical improvements, build engineering continues to present a range of enduring and emergent challenges. These arise from the growing complexity of software systems, diversification of programming paradigms, and evolving demands imposed by cloud-native development and large-scale deployment environments. While modern build systems have advanced in areas such as parallelism, caching, and incremental builds, several foundational problems remain open or only partially addressed. These problems create fertile ground for future innovation within the community.

A primary challenge lies in attaining *deterministic build behavior* across increasingly complex and heterogeneous environments. Determinism ensures that a given set of source inputs, configuration files, and dependency versions always produce bitwise-identical build outputs. This property is critical for reproducibility, debugging, and security. However, non-determinism can creep in from multiple sources:

- implicit dependencies on system libraries and environment variables,

- timestamp variations,

- race conditions in parallel builds, and

- nondeterministic code generators or compilation tools.

Existing solutions use hermetic sandboxing, content-addressable storage, and strict dependency declaration protocols, but fully eliminating all side channels remains arduous. Moreover, the explosion of containerized and distributed build infrastructures adds new dimensions of variability that must be controlled.

Another important open area is *cross-language integration within build systems*. Modern software products often combine components written in different languages, each with its own unique ecosystem of build tools, dependency managers, and compilation pipelines. Coordinating these heterogeneous workflows to produce unified artifacts, while preserving correctness and performance, is nontrivial. Current build tools either layer language-specific build steps with custom glue code or rely on monolithic all-encompassing systems that may lack flexibility and agility. Challenges arise in:

- capturing accurate cross-language dependencies at fine granularity,

- managing transitive dependency conflicts, and

- supporting mixed-language incremental builds that avoid unnecessary recompilation.

Furthermore, language-specific tools frequently evolve independently, complicating integration. A unified but extensible meta-build framework that harmonizes disparate language toolchains while retaining scalability is a key open problem.

Scaling build systems to *massive monolithic codebases*-often comprising tens of millions of lines distributed across thousands of developers-remains a critical concern. Such scale stresses all aspects of build engineering: dependency graph management, caching infrastructure, distributed build execution, and incremental build correctness. Even with optimized algorithms, tracking and invalidating dependencies accurately can overwhelm both build servers and developer machines. Network bandwidth and storage throughput become bottlenecks due to large artifact sizes and cache synchronization costs. The dynamic nature of enormous codebases exacerbates these issues, as frequent changes ripple through dependency graphs in unforeseen ways. Redesigning build systems to exploit locality and modularity at unprecedented levels, and to integrate seamlessly with code review and CI/CD workflows, is a vibrant research frontier.

In addition to these core areas, the rise of *polyglot environments*, *cloud-native continuous integration*, and *edge computing* introduces new complexity. Build systems must adapt to ephemeral infrastructure, heterogeneous target platforms, and rapidly evolving deployment topologies. Incorporating machine learning techniques for build optimization, auto-tuning, and fault prediction is promising but immature. Improving user and developer experience through better diagnostics, visualization, and automated dependency inference remains an open design space.

These challenges exemplify the need for continued collaboration between academia and industry to devise new abstractions, algorithms, and architectures that reconcile scalability, correctness, and usability. Open problems in build engineering offer rich opportunities for innovation:

- formal models ensuring determinism,

- standardized protocols for cross-language dependency specification, and

- distributed incremental build frameworks designed specifically for large-scale polyglot repositories.

Advancing build systems will not only accelerate software delivery but also improve software quality, security, and maintainability at scale, underscoring their critical role in the software engineering ecosystem.

9.5. Evolving Standards and Community Practices

The ecosystem surrounding Bazel has undergone significant maturation, marked by an evolving landscape of rule repositories, best practices, and governance models. As the system's user base and scope have expanded, so too have the mechanisms through which community knowledge, tooling, and standards are curated and disseminated. This evolution necessitates a proactive strategy for monitoring changes and integrating new standards to ensure that build configurations remain both robust and forward-compatible.

Originally, Bazel's core capabilities were supplemented by a modest set of externally maintained "rules" enabling support for diverse languages and platforms. Over time, these rule sets have converged towards a more standardized and modular architecture, reflecting both user demand for consistency and the community's efforts at consolidation. The rules_bazel organization on

GitHub now serves as a centralized hub for official and community-curated rule sets, such as `rules_go`, `rules_java`, `rules_docker`, and `rules_nodejs`. Each repository adheres to rigorous compatibility and deprecation policies, often coordinated through Bazel's Tooling Working Group to ensure harmonization.

Rule authors have incorporated semantic versioning and CI-driven testing matrices to guarantee predictable integration paths. Governance of these repositories typically involves maintainers elected or recognized by the community, with transparent roadmaps and issue tracking. Importantly, the shift towards "workspace delegation" has facilitated more granular updates, enabling users to adopt improvements incrementally without wholesale disruptive changes.

Best practices in Bazel usage have likewise evolved from anecdotal and site-specific heuristics into documented, codified guidelines. The Bazel community has invested considerably in maintaining comprehensive style guides, deterministic build principles, and performance optimization techniques. Some prominent trends include:

- **Rule Composition and Reuse**: Emphasis on defining composable macros and repository rules to abstract complexity and encourage reuse.

- **Strict Dependency Management**: Enforcing explicit dependencies and minimal transitive closure to reduce rebuild scope and improve reliability.

- **Sandboxing and Hermeticity**: Adoption of sandboxed execution environments and strict hermetic inputs to maximize cache hits and build reproducibility.

- **Error Reporting and Debuggability**: Standardization of messaging formats and debugging aids in rule implementations.

Documentation of these practices is maintained both in official Bazel repositories and community-curated knowledge bases, such as Bazel's discourse forums, Stack Overflow tags, and curated blogs. The design and maintenance of these resources underscore the necessity of continuous engagement with evolving conventions as well as active participation in community discussions to share insights and adopt innovations promptly.

Bazel's governance structure embraces an open governance model centered around the Bazel team at Google and a broad base of external contributors and users. The significance of community input is reflected in working groups established to steward specific focus areas, including user experience, rules development, and performance enhancement. These groups operate through transparent RFC (Request for Comments) processes and weekly community meetings documented publicly.

Governance practices highlight the importance of maintaining stable APIs, providing deprecation windows that allow downstream users to adapt, and employing compatibility testing across versions. The Bazel release cycle incorporates staged rollouts and continuous integration to minimize regressions.

For adopters of Bazel within enterprises or large organizations, establishing internal governance aligned with community standards is critical. This involves formulating internal policies on Bazel version upgrades, rules repository synchronization, and custom rule auditing to ensure compliance with both upstream changes and organizational requirements.

To keep build systems future-proof in the face of continual evolution, practitioners must institute mechanisms for monitoring community developments and integrating standards promptly:

- **Subscribe to Official Channels**: Engaging with Bazel's mailing lists, GitHub notifications on core and rules repositories, and community forums provides early visibility into emerging proposals and deprecations.

- **Regularly Audit Dependencies**: Automated tooling to analyze and report on rule and dependency versions facilitates timely upgrades and vulnerability assessments.

- **Incremental Migration Strategies**: Employing feature flags, parallel build configurations, or shadow builds allows for testing new standards without risking build breakages.

- **Participate in Community Feedback**: Contributing to RFC discussions and providing real-world feedback accelerates the refinement cycle and aligns expectations.

Technically, continuous integration pipelines can be enhanced to include validation against the latest released rules and Bazel versions. Adoption of tools like bazelisk can simplify version management by automating Bazel binary selection. Additionally, defining policies to handle deprecation notices-typically communicated months in advance-enables teams to schedule preparatory refactoring in manageable increments.

Consider the upgrade path for rules_go from version 0.29 to 0.30. The following snippet shows how the repository definition in the WORKSPACE file is updated:

```
http_archive(
    name = "io_bazel_rules_go",
    urls = ["https://github.com/bazelbuild/rules_go/releases/
    download/v0.30.0/rules_go-v0.30.0.tar.gz"],
    sha256 = "
    abcdef1234567890abcdef1234567890abcdef1234567890abcdef1234567890
    ",
)
```

The release notes for rules_go provide details on new features, deprecated attributes, and recommended migration steps. By integrating automation that monitors these releases and schedules the necessary changes, build maintainers can ensure compatibility and leverage performance or functionality improvements promptly.

The continual refinement of Bazel's rule repositories, best practices, and governance structures reflects its dynamic and collaborative development ethos. Keeping abreast of these developments through systematic tracking, engagement, and incremental adoption is essential to sustaining performant and maintainable build systems over the long term.

www.ingramcontent.com/pod-product-compliance
Lightning Source LLC
Chambersburg PA
CBHW061245220326
41599CB00028B/5538